FAMILY RESTORATION 1

POWER MUST CHANGE HANDS
Vol. 5

Godson T. Nembo

IEM PRESS

FAMILY RESTORATION 1
Power Must Change Hands Vol. 5

Copyright © September 2015

Godson T. Nembo

All rights reserved.

ISBN: 978-1-947662-26-1

For more information:
www.christianrestorationnetwork.org

www.facebook.com/godsontnembo

Email: info@christianrestorationnetwork.org

Or write to:
Tangumonkem Godson Nembo

P.O. Box 31339 Biyem Assi Yaounde – Cameroon

Tel.: (237) 674.495.895 or 699.902.618

IEM PRESS is honored to present this title with the author. The views expressed or implied in this work are those of the author. IEM Press provides our imprint seal representing design excellence, creative content and high quality production. To learn more about IEM Press visit www.iempublishing.com

otherwise—without the prior permission of the copyright holder, except as provided by USA copyright law.

CONTENTS

INTRODUCTION

Welcome to another edition of *"Power Must Change Hands."* Power Must Change Hands 30 Days Annual Fast has become a yearly prophetic event which gathers God's people from around Cameroon and beyond for 30 days of power. Every year during this program God's power brings supernatural turnarounds in the lives of individuals and families. Many thrilling testimonies were recorded during past editions. This year, the Almighty God will move again mightily among us.

The prophetic message the Lord gave me for this edition is *"Family Restoration."* During the annual fast to take over the year 2015, the Lord told me that this year I should focus on families because He wants to begin a great work of restoration in families. From January till now I have gone to different villages to carry out family deliverance. We burnt idols and shrines and broke curses on families. Some of them recorded immediate results.

Many families in the land are languishing under curses and demonic yokes. Some of them do not even know that they are bound. Others who are aware that they are under attack aggravate the situation by turning to witchdoctors for help. Still others who believe that God can help them out of their predicament do organize prayer programs to seek the face of God for family breakthroughs but lack tools for effective prayer. This book is written to serve as a prayer manual for deliverance and restoration at personal and family levels.

Through the direction of the Holy Spirit I have developed key topics that should guide every user to identify the root causes of some common spiritual problems that are tormenting families and how to deal with them prayerfully and practically. As you read and pray through this book, get ready for supernatural encounters with the transforming power of God.

Prayer and fasting releases a spiritual force that breaks all types of spiritual barriers and ushers in God's multidimensional blessings on individuals, families and nations. During the next 30 days on the "Mountain of Restoration," the anointing that brings deliverance, revival and restoration will be activated mightily for supernatural breakthroughs on individuals, families, Churches and even our nation.

You have been divinely connected to the "Prayer Storm" anointing in this season because God is determined to bring a turnaround in your life. One of the blessings of our ministry is supernatural angelic ministrations. As you pray fervently, angels will be released for your restoration.

God bless you and your family as you go through this prayer journey.

Tangumonkem Godson Nembo,
Bamenda, August 2015

Part 1:

PREPARING TO PRAY

Chapter 1

HOW TO USE THIS BOOK

It is a Prayer Guide

The most important thing I want you to know is that this book is called "A prayer guide" and not a novel. It is not meant to be read like other books; it should be used to pray. The book does not pray for you but it directs you on how to pray effectively. If you only read it and do not pray through it, you may not benefit anything from it. I have received exciting testimonies from people who used my books to pray. I didn't even pray for them but they encountered the power of God as they used the books.

Use this book as follows:

1. Always read the message of the day and all the scriptures before you start to pray.
2. As you go along, the Holy Spirit may impress certain burdens on your heart. Focus on them as you pray. You

may not have to pray every prayer point I have written down in this book. Pray as the Holy Spirit guides you.

3. Do not pray the prayers in your heart; pray them audibly, but not so loud that you disturb anyone. Sometimes you have to look for a conducive environment where you can freely pour out your heart to God f without disturbing anyone. You can go to your church or to any other prayer ground.

4. Some people just read the prayer points and end with, "In the name of Jesus, Amen!" This is not the right way to pray your way to breakthrough. Whenever you read a prayer point, keep the book aside and take some time to pray it through before you read the next one.

5. If you can pray in tongues, always allow the Holy Spirit to pray through you as you work with this book.

6. You are not obliged to pray all the prayers on a particular day or during one prayer session. You can stop somewhere and then continue later.

7. You can also pick out topics from this book and use to carry out a 1 day fast, 3 days, 7 days, 21 days fast or even a 40 days fast.

8. Pastors, prayer cell leaders, ministry heads, etc., can use this book to lead their groups in seasons of fasting and prayer. I have had many pastors who used the previous editions of this book to run fasting programs for their churches and the results were awesome. These programs ranged from 7 days to 30 days.

9. If your health condition does not permit you to fast now, you can also take a 30 days' journey of intense prayer with the book and you will still be blessed.

10. Believe God that the grace and the anointing that is active

on God's servant will visit you as you work with this book. **Note:** Do the *Prophetic Thanksgiving Prayers* in Chapter 7 before you begin praying every day. Also round every day with the *Prophetic Declarations* in Chapter 8.

Focus on the Solution and not on the Problem

I have received uncountable messages from people who read *Power Must Change Hands*. Most of them read, "O pastor I now know that the problem I have been suffering from is a spiritual problem." Some read, "Pastor, I have discovered the spirit that has been tormenting me." One old man visited me one day and told me with excitement that "The strongman has died." When I tried to find out from him who the strongman he was talking about was, he told me that it was a certain family member who had just died.

The purpose of writing this book is twofold: First, to try to expose, as the Lord gives us light, the root causes of some of the spiritual problems we are facing; and second, to propose some solutions to these problems. If you focus only on the cause of the problem and keep talking about it, you will never be free. But if you identify the solution to that problem and focus on it, your deliverance and breakthrough will be established. For example, if your marriage is crumbling and you have done all in vain to put things in order, and then someone comes to you offering to help, and says, "I have a solution to your marital problem, and it is that I see a spirit husband sowing confusion between you and your spouse", it could be true that the force responsible for your marital problems is a spirit husband. But then your question would be, "How do I deal with this spirit husband for peace to return to my home?" When the cause of a problem is exposed, the problem is partly solved. Until you lay hold on the solution, you cannot solve the problem. Nowadays, people run around looking for someone to prophesy to them. Actually, some prophets even announce that they have the ability to give "Microscopic prophecies." If the "Microscopic prophecy" can describe your problem and its root cause in microscopic detail but fails to present a "Microscopic solution," then it is just soothsaying – "Ngambi."

So, as you read this book, do not only try to find out the cause of your problems, always underline the solutions proposed and focus on them. Also listen to the leading of the Holy Spirit on what to do. Note this:

"You are in bondage because you or someone before you did the wrong thing. That bondage will be broken when you or someone after you decides to begin to do the right thing."

For example, a curse comes when someone breaks the law of God by committing a lawless act like incest, murder, homosexuality, or extortion. To break the curse and turn it to a blessing, one must repent, carry out restitution, and then begin to live a holy life.

Chapter 2

INSTRUCTIONS TO FOLLOW AS YOU FAST

These practical steps will guide you as you engage in the fast. Read through carefully and endeavour to follow the instructions.

1. Set a definite period for your fast. Will your fast be for 3 days, 7 days, 21 days, 30 days or more? Tell yourself, "I am going to fast for . . . days." Do this to avoid being discouraged by the devil along the journey. If the Lord leads you to add the number of days as you progress in the fast, do not hesitate, but obey.

2. This fast is supposed to be broken every evening after prayer unless God leads you otherwise.

3. Set aside enough time to pray in the morning and in the evening. Join one of the different groups that are meeting to pray in your locality. If there is no such group, locate a prayer partner. If there is none, pray alone.

4. Drink a lot of water during the fast. Experts say that everyone should drink at least 3 litres of water a day. So during this time, drink more than 3 litres. The water will help to cleanse your body. To make this very effective, always squeeze some drops of lemon juice into the water.

5. Do not engage in excessive work or exercise during the fast.

6. Spend much time praying, reading and meditating on the word of God without which your fast could become simply a hunger strike or starvation. On the last page I have included a program to read through the New Testament or the Gospels in 30 days. Attempt it.

7. Use the prayer points in this book as a guide but also add yours as the Holy Spirit leads you.

8. Pray the word of God. Do this by using Bible verses to reinforce your prayers.

9. Be attentive to what the Holy Spirit is saying and make sure you note it in your diary. Write down all the visions, dreams and prophecies God gives you during this time. You have to write them down because you may forget, or the devil could steal them from you.

10. Settle any disputes before you start to fast. Disputes, bitterness and un-forgiveness will block your prayers from reaching God. During and after the fast avoid quarrels and arguments.

11. Do not go around announcing to everyone that you are fasting (Matt.6:16-17).

12. Wash yourself and be clean. Brush your teeth regularly and also use perfume if possible (there are bad odours released from the body during fasting). Rinse your mouth with salty water; add a small amount of baking powder or

lemon juice into the water.

13. Do not focus on your body weaknesses (the body is just reacting to the absence of food). Keep telling yourself, "It is well, I am an eagle, I will make it to the end!"

14. Pray with expectation. God will never let you seek Him in vain.

15. Make sacrifices (gifts and helps) during and after your fast.

16. Break the fast every day with a lot of care. Do not over eat or mix many different types of foods (even fruits). You can use only fruits to break your fast on some of the days. Drink a lot of water.

17. Should you encounter any difficulty, meet and talk to your spiritual leader or to someone who is very experienced in fasting.

18. Regarding sex during a fast, the Bible says:

"Do not deprive one another except with consent for a time, that you may give yourselves to fasting and prayer; and come together again so that Satan does not tempt you because of your lack of self-control" (1Cor.7:5).

It is not a sin for a married couple to have sexual relations during a fast when the two are in agreement. It is wrong to deprive your spouse without his/her consent. It is best to stay away from sex in order to focus on the Lord. Let the Holy Spirit guide you.

Chapter 3

THE POWER OF FASTING

To "fast" simply means to abstain from food in order to focus on God in prayer. If you refuse to eat and do not pray, we call that a "hunger strike" or starvation, and not fasting. I pray that during this season you shall fast and not be on a hunger strike or starvation.

The spiritual power that is released through fasting and prayer can only be likened to A*tomic Power*. Those who know how to tap this power are doing exploits. As a minister of the Gospel for more than eighteen years now, I have experienced uncommon miracles and breakthroughs through the power of fasting, both in my life and in the lives of others.

Even Satanists exploit the power of fasting in order to tap into satanic power. I read in one of Dr. Peter Wagner's books that some years ago Satanists gathered in the nation of South Africa to fast for the destruction of the families of believers. It was reported that after the fast, many marriages of believers and even those of some top Ministers of the Gospel collapsed woefully. A few years ago I prayed with a girl from Bafoussam – Cameroon, who told me that she once fasted for 40 days just to acquire evil powers to destroy some families. After her fast, she killed some people mysteriously, including even her own family members. I also read the testimony of a man who fasted for one year in order to be able to have a personal encounter with Lucifer. After that, he became a very destructive occultist.

Other religious adherents like Buddhists, Hindus and Moslems also fast regularly. Medical practitioners recommend fasting for the cleansing of the body. A woman told me some years ago that her doctor placed her on a three day fast, after which she regained her health without drugs.

Even animals practice fasting. When the caterpillar prepares to transition to the next stage (butterfly), it goes into a season of fasting. The eagle also fasts in order to improve on its ability to fly higher; and so on. Snakes fast when they want to shed their skin in order to grow fatter. You too can fast.

In the year 2001 the Lord gave me this mandate to fast for 30 days every year to pray for a move of God in the church. By the grace of God, I have been doing it faithfully till today. And then in 2010 He spoke to me clearly that I should invite others to connect to the blessing. As at now, thousands of people around the world join me yearly for the 30 days fast. The results are awesome.

Types of Fasts

Normal Fast: This involves abstaining from all solid and liquid food with the exception of water.

Absolute Fast: This involves abstaining from both food and drink. You should never fast for more than three days without water unless under the special direction of the Holy Spirit.

Daniel Fast: This consists of eating only fruits, vegetables, and drinking water.

What Fasting does

"But those who wait on the LORD shall renew their strength; They shall mount up with wings like eagles, They shall run and not be weary, They shall walk and not faint. (Isa.40:31).

1. Fasting serves to subject our bodies to our spirits so that we can receive from the Holy Spirit (ICor.9:27).
2. Fasting is disciplining the body, mind, and spirit so that we can focus on God in order to tap into His riches (Prov.25:28).
3. Fasting is subordinating our fleshly desires to the desires of the Holy Spirit so that the life of God can overshadow us (Gal.5:17).
4. Fasting helps us set priorities in our lives. By fasting we place God in the first place in our lives as we subdue our fleshly desires (Mat.6:33).
5. Fasting draws us very close to God (Ps.63:1-2).

Why Fast?

Fasting is the greatest spiritual discipline needed for seeking God's intervention. Combined with prayer they together make up the most critical weapons of spiritual warfare and deliverance in our lives. While we cannot manipulate God to fulfill our desires, fasting always (when done the biblical way) moves God to fulfill his intended will over issues concerning us. So we fast to:

1. Honor God - Matt.6:16-18; Luke 2:37; Acts 13:2; Mat.5:6
2. Humble ourselves before God - 2Chron.7:14-15
3. To seek God for divine healing - I Cor.11:30; Jam.5:13-18, Isa.59:1-2
4. To seek deliverance from Bondages – Mat.17:21; Isa.58:6-9 (loose bands of wickedness).
5. To seek God for revelation - God's vision and will – Dan.9:3, 20-21; Dan.10:2-10, 12-13
6. To seek God for personal or corporate revival- Acts 1:4, 14; Acts 2:16-21, Joel 2:12-18
7. To repent from personal failures – Ps.51; Jer.29:11-14, Jam.4:8-10

Unfortunately, nowadays few Christians take fasting seriously. If we all would fast as revealed in the Bible, there would be great revivals the world over, breaking of bondages (yokes) in our lives and in other people's lives. We also would be able to hear from God more clearly.

"Is not this the fast that I Choose: to loose the bonds of wickedness, to undo the things of the yoke, to let the oppressed go free, and to break every yoke? .... Then shall you call, and the Lord will answer; you shall cry,

and he will say, here I am," (Isa.58:6-7, 9).

10 Helpful Reminders About Fasting

1. Fasting will not Kill you

Throughout history, fasting has been a prescribed method of healing. Hippocrates was an outstanding physician in his time and is called the "Father of Modern Medicine." He set standards followed by doctors today called the Hippocratic Oath. Hippocrates personally fasted and taught his students to rely on diet and exercise instead of drugs.

2. Consult a medical doctor if you have health problems

Do not engage in a serious fast without getting appropriate medical advice if you have a challenging health condition like diabetes, pregnancy, etc. If you can meet a Christian medical doctor who has practical experience in fasting, it would be good. Before you fast, I repeat, meet a medical doctor if you have a challenging health problem.

3. Headaches, bad breath, and feelings of tiredness indicate that your fast is working

During times of fasting the body purifies itself and releases impurities and body toxins from your body. This often causes bad breath and body odors.

4. Fasting strengthens man's inner will

James 1:7-8 says, **"A double minded man is unstable in all his ways. Let not that man think that he will receive anything from the Lord."**

Do all in your power to not break your fast when you feel

hunger pangs. The only reasons you can have to break your fast are: if God speaks to you to do so; if the time of the fast is over or for medical reasons.

5. Fasting increases a person's faith
Fasting and prayer will increase your faith.

6. Fasting is a method of constant intercession before God
Many times when a person fasts they do not feel like praying. Intercessory prayer is not only a spiritual but also a physical process. Sometimes during a fast one becomes weak and does not feel like praying. Remember, your fast is a constant prayer unto God.

7. During the fast you must focus on the Word of God
Most of the direction that God gives to His people comes from the revelation of His Word. When Jesus fasted, He was tempted by the devil, but in every case He used the word of God to overcome him. When you become hungry, read the Word of God.

8. During the fast, let your prayers be specific
Pray for the specific reasons why the fast was called. Write down your greatest needs and specifically pray over each one of them. As God gives you instructions and guidance, write down what He is saying.

9. Wisdom must be used in breaking the fast
Never use hard food to break your fast. In the case of a complete fast lasting more than 3 days, do not break it with

meat. Eat meat after some days. Eat easy to digest foods. The sooner the first meal passes through your body the greater the effect it has in carrying out poisons collected in your intestines and stomach during the fast. The best laxative foods are fresh, sweet fruits, carrots or raw vegetables.

10. Your victory often comes after your fast

Many times the answers to the prayers you are praying begin to manifest in the days following your fast. This was the case with Jesus after His fast (Luke 4:14).

Join the Fast!

Experience has proven that it is easier to fast with other people than doing it alone. During this season of fasting, there is a corporate anointing you can tap into. So connect now!

You may not be able to fast for 30 days but you can start from somewhere. A Chinese proverb says, "The journey of 1000 km begins with a step." As you step out in faith the Lord will strengthen you. I know many people who had come across other volumes of *"Power Must Change Hands"* and decided to use them to fast and pray. Even though they prayed alone and during a different period, God still visited them and gave them great breakthroughs.

Let me end this section by saying that fasting has a very important role to play in the accomplishment of your destiny. I challenge you, go out there and carry out a study of all the men and women who created an impact in their generations, from the Old Testament till today. You will discover one thing common to all of them. The word is "Discipline." All of them without any exception disciplined themselves to fast. The only exception should have been Jesus Christ, who was the son of God. But He fasted even more than most of them. If Jesus fasted, why do you think you should not fast? Join the fast!

"Declare a holy fast; call a sacred assembly. Summon the elders and all who live in the land to the house of the LORD your God, and cry out to the LORD" (Joel 1:14).

Just as it was in the days of Joel, the LORD is using me to blow the trumpet and call a fast because he wants to do a great work among His people.

"Then the LORD will be zealous for His land, And pity His people. . . So I will restore to you the years that the swarming locust has eaten . . ." (Joel 2:18, 25).

We cannot be at ease in Zion because a lot is going wrong in our lives, the Church and in the nation. We must arise and seek the LORD for the fulfilment of His word in our midst.

Chapter 4

HOW TO FIGHT SPIRITUAL BATTLES

I have observed that many people in our times are trying to fight spiritual battles with carnal weapons. It is for this reason that I think we should understand how to fight spiritual battles before we go into serious prayers. Anyone who goes into a battle without the appropriate knowledge ends up a casualty or a captive. In this chapter I want to expose to you the basic information you need before you engage in the battle.

Spiritual Battles are Fought With Spiritual Weapons

The Bible makes it crystal clear that spiritual battles should NEVER be fought with carnal (physical) weapons because:

Our enemies are spiritual enemies:

The enemies you are engaging in the battle are not physical enemies, they are spiritual.

"For we are not fighting against flesh and blood enemies, but against evil rulers and authorities of the unseen world, against mighty powers in this dark world, and against evil spirits in the heavenly places" (Eph.6:12) NLT.

Whenever you misrepresent your enemy in a battle, you are exposed to disaster. The devil knows this very well and what he tries to do is to cause you to direct your weapons against the wrong enemy.

A family came to me once and told me that they had finally discovered that the person responsible for the calamities that had been rampant in their family was a certain neighbor. When I asked them about the source of the revelation, they told me that a certain witchdoctor revealed it to them. I always tell people that I can never build on any revelation that comes through a servant of the devil. These agents of Satan called witchdoctors and soothsayers have torn apart many families through such demonic revelations. In fact, if God has a revelation for me and it must come through a witchdoctor, I pray that He should never send any of them to me. He can use a donkey or a raven to speak to me, but not a witchdoctor. These people told me that they were going to physically attack the wizard in question. I told them that spiritual battles are never fought like that. I told them that if the man was actually the one responsible for the deaths of members of their family then we would have to deal with the devil that was using him. Please, do not go out there to quarrel and fight with anybody in the name of spiritual warfare.

You have to learn to separate the enemy from the instrument. Behind every evil man or woman is a spirit. It is the spirit (witchcraft, sorcery, rape, incest, murder, occult, etc.) in the person that makes him or her evil. Reflect on this: if somebody came against you with a sharp cutlass and you had a gun, what would be your target; the man or the cutlass? A wise person would aim at the man. If your bullet got the man, the cutlass would fall off. Whenever we succeed to arrest the spirit using an individual, we win the battle, and sometimes the person is even won to the Lord. Look at this scripture:

"But He turned and said to Peter, "Get behind Me, Satan! You are an offense to Me, for you are not mindful of the things of God, but the things of men" (Mat.16:23).

In this Bible verse, Jesus rebuked Peter very sharply. A careful look at the verse reveals that, "Get behind me Satan" was addressed to the spirit that was using Peter at that time and not to Peter. Jesus went on to straighten Peter's corrupt mind by saying that,

"If anyone desires to come after Me, let him deny himself, and take up his cross, and follow Me" (Mat.16:24).

Doesn't it surprise you that instead of Jesus calling down fire to kill Peter, He instead rebuked the devil who was using him, and then went on to teach him?

It is sad today that whenever we sense the hand of the

devil in someone's life resisting us, we call on the fire of God to consume the person. This is the same thing James and John needed Jesus' permission to do in Samaria. Hear what they said,

"Lord, do You want us to command fire to come down from heaven and consume them, just as Elijah did?" (Luke 9:54).

They were nicknamed "Sons of thunder." Today we have many "Sons and daughters of thunder and fire" in the Church of Jesus Christ. What was Jesus' response?

"But He turned and rebuked them, and said, "You do not know what manner of spirit you are of. 'For the Son of Man did not come to destroy men's lives but to save them.' And they went to another village" (Luke 9:55-56).

We are of another spirit – the Spirit of Christ. We are not terrorists. We must do ministry following the pattern of our master Jesus Christ.

Once I visited a big Church on a Sunday morning and heard the pastor say during the prayer time, "Write down the names of all your enemies and bring to the altar and let's judge them." I saw people writing lists of names and taking to the pastor. He put the pieces of paper in a box and began to call curses and destruction on whosoever's name was in the box as he poured olive oil on them. I call this "Charismatic witchcraft."

Please pray against evil spirits as revealed in the Bible. Bind them and destroy their works in the lives of people and territories assigned to you by God. Do not waste your time praying that evil spirits should die. Do not also pray that people should die. The Bible records many testimonies of the enemies of God's people who were judged by God to death. When you read the Bible carefully you find out that the early Christians did not pray that God should kill their enemies. God struck Herod to death, as well as those who wanted to kill Jesus when He was born (Acts 12:21-24, Mat.2:20). The question is, Did Joseph and Mary pray that God should kill all those who were after Jesus' life? I think the answer is no. Paul could have killed the magician Bar-Jesus who was obstructing his ministry openly but he asked blindness on him for a season (Acts 13:8-10). Jesus did not pray for anyone's death, and neither did Paul. They rather prayed for their deliverance from these wicked men.

"And that we may be delivered from unreasonable and wicked men; for not all have faith" (2Thes.3:2).

God alone has the power to punish with death whosoever He wants. Our duty is to pray violently against evil spirits and the evil works of evil men. I think that if we could engage in spiritual warfare like the early Church did we should see great manifestations of God's power among us. I think it is ignorance, fear or immaturity that leads people to pray those "extra-biblical" and "anti-spiritual" prayers. I am not trying to argue that evil spirits and agents of darkness are not causing havoc in the world. But should all of them be killed by fire? Weren't some of us full time agents of darkness? What if the Church had prayed you to death, would you be a worshipper of Jesus Christ today? There are many anointed children of God in Churches today who were terrible witches and wizards in the past. I know of a lady who in the past was a witch and had killed many people. t. She tried to sacrifice her mother and her brother who were both believers but failed. The witch coven decided to kill her so she ran to Jesus Christ and was delivered. Today she is serving the Lord fervently.

The proponents of "Suffer not a witch to live" or "kill all the witches," quote **Exodus 22:18, *"Thou shalt not suffer a witch to live."*** Under the Old Testament what this verse meant was that the witch should be stoned to death. Remember that adulterers and fornicators were also condemned to death by this same OT law.

"The man who commits adultery with another man's wife, …, the adulterer and the adulteress, shall surely be put to death" (Lev.20:10).

So if you believe in "Suffer not the witch to live," then also apply the rule on the adulterers and fornicators. Add in your prayers "Suffer not the adulterers and the fornicators to live. Let them die by fire!"

I learnt a lesson:

Something happened to me that changed my mindset concerning praying that fire should destroy people. During the annual 30 days fast in October 2013, a Muslim man came to our Church to attack me because his concubine was attending the prayer sessions. I did not even know that the lady was participating in the program. A few days before the incident, the Holy Spirit was talking to me very strongly on developing a merciful heart. I remember that I prayed a number of times that God should give me a merciful heart. That day we were deep in prayer in Church when suddenly I felt that somebody was standing before me at the altar where I was. When I opened my eyes, I saw a man with a hand lifted up to strike me. I shouted "Stop in Jesus' name!" and he became immobilized. I called the ushers to take him out. He was fuming with anger as they dragged him away from the altar. As soon as he left, the whole place began to stink. I was told later that the man had smoked marijuana and was holding a lit cigarette when he came to attack me at the altar.

He told my elders who tried to find out why he came to attack me that he did it deliberately. He said that as a Muslim one cannot do that in a mosque. He wanted to desecrate our church and then strike me down. When I heard all this at the end of the prayer session, I became furious. I vowed that the man must know that he had stepped on fire. As soon as I got home I went to my place of prayer to deal with him. The Holy Spirit spoke to me very clearly, "Remember mercy." I thought of what God had been teaching me that week on mercy and I was broken. All I said was, "Lord, take over." The next day when I arrived the Church compound, the man and his concubine were there waiting for me. He broke down and began to beg me to forgive him. I told him I had forgiven him. He begged to apologize to the Church. During the service that evening, he came to the platform and pleaded that God and the people should forgive him. He said he would like to be a pastor like me. We led him to Jesus and prayed for him. What do you think would have happened to this man if I spent that evening calling down fire upon him?

A lot of errors are creeping into the body of Christ in our times. Some of these strange teachings and practices are accepted by naïve Church members without cross-examination. Take note, your enemy is the devil and evil spirits. Any human being opposing and fighting your destiny or the will of God for your family and community is an instrument in the hands of the devil. Identify the spirit behind the person. Bind it and cast it away. Destroy their works and begin to establish the kingdom of God prophetically. Let God be the one to choose to kill someone, not you. Here is what the Word says,

"If it is possible, as much as depends on you, live peaceably with all men. Beloved, do not avenge yourselves, but rather give place to wrath; for it is written, "Vengeance is Mine, I will repay," says the Lord" (Rom.12:18-19).

Our weapons are spiritual weapons:

If from my explanation you have understood that your enemies are spiritual and not physical then you should automatically use spiritual weapons to confront them. At the close of this chapter, I will introduce you to some spiritual weapons of warfare you need for your battles. But for now I want the truth that, "Spiritual enemies can only be fought with spiritual weapons" to sink deep into your spirit.

"We are humans, but we don't wage war as humans do. We use God's mighty weapons, not worldly weapons, to knock down the strongholds of human reasoning and to destroy false arguments" (2Cor.10:3-4) NLT.

It is clear from this scripture that the weapons we need for spiritual battles are spiritual weapons. The above verse calls the weapons, *"God's mighty weapons."* God has made available mighty weapons to enable you fight and win your battles against the forces of darkness.

You will also notice in the scripture we are dealing with that the weapons of the enemy are *"Strongholds of human reasonings and false arguments."* So the fight against the forces of darkness is first a "Mental battle." Spiritual warfare is basically "psychological warfare." The devil knows this and that is why his target is to cause us to believe the wrong thing. Whenever he succeeds to capture one's mind, it becomes easy for him to destroy that individual. That is why the first piece of armor God has provided for our defense is the belt of truth (Eph.6:14). Jesus said in John 8:32, **"And you shall know the truth, and the truth shall make you free."** You must equip yourself with the truth of God's word to be able to stand against the forces of darkness. Until you conquer the spirits in your mind, you cannot destroy their works.

When you observe how some people engage the forces of darkness in warfare, you realize that they are not praying from the stand point of the knowledge of God's word, but from fear. A study of the armor of God in Ephesians 6:14-17 shows that we have one offensive weapon called the "Sword of the Spirit" which is the word of God. Our major defensive weapon is the "Shield of faith." The word of God is therefore your major defense equipment and also your weapon of attack. People resort to carnal weapons just because they lack the word of God in their spirits. How do you explain the fact that a Christian is exchanging blows with someone because he/she believes that the person is an agent of the devil? Do we box demons out of people? Today, it is common to see people engage in spiritual warfare with all sorts of objects. Some people literally carry cutlasses and swords to fight the battle. In one of such Churches, members literally run out of the Church with sharp cutlasses and will begin to chop down trees saying that the evil spirits have entered those trees. The same objects that witchdoctors use for their art are gradually coming into the Church.

We must awake from sleep. If you will win your spiritual battles, learn to do it the way Jesus did. Follow the pattern of the Apostles. In 1Timothy 6:12, Apostle Paul calls the spiritual battles we are facing, "The fight of faith." It is fought based on the word of God. A couple who came to me for prayers a few years ago asked me, "Pastor, you just pray like that without giving anything?" These days prayer is being associated with many things. Some people even believe that prayers without additives do not work. Some of these additives or objects derail people's faith while others open people to demonic pollutions. So watch out. I encourage ministers of the gospel to watch out against people who would try to pressurize them to become syncretic. Syncretism is actually the attempt to mix up pure Christianity with African traditional practices.

The Weapons of Our Warfare

Here are weapons you need to employ as you engage the enemy in spiritual warfare:

1. Be born again – When you receive Jesus Christ as your personal Lord and Savior, you receive power to overcome demons.

"But as many as received Him, to them He gave the right to become children of God, to those who believe in His name" (Jn.1:12). Jesus who now dwells in you rebukes the enemies for you. (See Jude 1:9; Zech.3:2). *"He that is in us is greater than he (Satan) that is in the world" (1Jn.4:4).*

Because you have Jesus Christ in you, you have the upper hand. Always remind your enemy about who you are in

Christ.

2. The name of Jesus – The name of Jesus in the mouth of a true believer is a dangerous weapon against the forces of darkness.

"At the name of Jesus every knee should bow, of those in heaven, and of those on earth, and of those under the earth," (Philp.2:9). Call the name of Jesus and the enemy will bow (Jn.14:14).

3. Fervent prayer – When a believer prays fervently there is a release of miraculous power. *"The earnest prayer of a righteous person has great power and produces wonderful results" (Ja.5:16).* You must also learn to pray a lot in tongues (Eph.6:18).

4. Faith – Do you know that faith is a dangerous defensive and offensive weapon God has made available for us? That is why the Bible says,

"Above all, taking the shield of faith with which you will be able to quench all the fiery darts of the wicked one" (Eph.6:16).

"For whatever is born of God overcomes the world. And this is the victory that has overcome the world—our faith" (1Jn.5:4).

Whenever you engage the enemy in battle, learn to stand your ground and resist him.

5. The Word - (God's promises) - Ephesians 6:17 says, *"And take the helmet of salvation, and the sword of the Spirit, which is the word of God;"* There are more than

34.000 promises in the Bible that can be fulfilled in your life. Quote these promises as you pray. Remember that Jesus quoted scriptures when He confronted the devil in the wilderness (Luke 4:1-11).

6. The Blood of Jesus – (The finished work of the cross) - Revelation 12:11 says,

"And they overcame him by the blood of the Lamb and by the word of their testimony, and they did not love their lives to the death."

Always remind your enemy about his defeat on the cross through the death of Jesus Christ. Also learn to cancel all his strategies with the blood of Jesus Christ. Cover your entire life with the blood.

7. Testimony – (The declaration of your belief in Jesus and the mighty weapons God has given to us). Revelation 12:11 says,

"And they have defeated him because of the blood of the Lamb and because of their testimony. And they were not afraid to die."

Your confession is important. Speak the faith language. Look at the enemy in the face and declare your victory over him, in Jesus' name.

8. Angelic assistance – God has assigned angels to assist us in our battles.

"Are not all angels ministering spirits sent to serve those who will inherit salvation?" (Heb.1:14) NIV.

The angels are always ready to act on your behalf. Learn to ask heaven to release them to assist you. Do not pray to angels, instead ask the Father, in the name of Jesus to send you angels. They will come and deal with the forces of darkness that come against you. I have experienced the ministry of angels many times in my ministry. During one crusade, an angel appeared to one lady and took her to her father's compound in her village about 200 km away. Together with the angel they began to destroy some altars and shrines. She said she saw the whole place on fire. That day she was delivered completely from demonic harassment. Her pastor testified later that before that day, they had struggled many times in vain to deliver her. That evening by the ministry of the angel, her captivity was turned around.

9. Other weapons – The Lord has made available other weapons for our spiritual warfare. Isaiah 29:6 points out six other weapons of war we have at our disposal:

"You shall be visited and delivered by the Lord of hosts with THUNDER and EARTHQUAKE and GREAT NOISE, with WHIRLWIND and TEMPEST and the flame of a devouring FIRE.

Release these weapons as you begin to battle with the forces of darkness. You will experience tremendous breakthroughs.

The devil has no weapon for which God has not prepared an anti. Take time to master these weapons. Also memorize Bible verses that deal with the weapons of spiritual warfare.

Engaging the Enemy in the Battle

I am often embarrassed by the way some people pray even when things are rough. They pray as if they have another option if God should fail to answer them. You cannot fight the forces of darkness like that and expect to conquer them. You must pray fervently and violently. This does not mean that you should shout and disturb people. I am talking about a fervent spirit. This is how you should pray:

1. Be strong – *"Finally, my brethren, be strong in the Lord and in the power of His might (Eph.6:10).* This speaks of boldness and courage in your heart as you pray.

2. Be aggressive– *"For we WRESTLE not against flesh and blood,"* **(Eph.6:12).** In this verse, spiritual warfare is called "Wrestling." So if you are not strong and aggressive enough you may be defeated. The dictionary defines "Aggressive" as *"Pursuing one's aims and interests forcefully."* Jesus taught His disciples to be forceful in kingdom pursuit. This is what He said,

"And from the days of John the Baptist until now the kingdom of heaven suffers violence, and the violent take it by force" (Mat.11:12).
Be determined to take back by force all the devil has stolen from your family, in Jesus' name.

3. Be firm – *"Therefore take up the whole armor of God, that you may be able to WITHSTAND in the evil day, and having done all, to STAND" (Eph.6:13).*
To be firm means to be determined and not ready to surrender no matter what. You should never surrender to Satan and his forces when you engage in the battle.

4. Resist him firmly– *"Therefore submit to God. Resist the devil and he will flee from you" (Ja.4:7).* To resist means to fight on and refuse to give up.

5. Bind him confidently– *"And I will give you the keys of the kingdom of heaven, and whatever you BIND on earth will be bound in heaven, and whatever you loose on earth will be loosed in heaven" (Mat.16:19).*
This means that you have to open your mouth and bind the devil audibly. Some people mistakenly think that it is more spiritual to pray in their hearts. Pray audibly.

6. Command him to leave – *"Then Jesus said to him, "Away with you, Satan! For it is written, 'You shall worship the LORD your God, and Him only you shall serve" (Mat.4:10).*
Just like Jesus did to the devil, you must learn to command the forces of darkness to leave. Take note that you do not give orders in your thoughts, you must do that audibly and forcefully.

7. Rebuke him firmly and sharply – *"And Jesus rebuked the demon, and it came and the child was cured from that very hour" (Mat.17:18).*
Every believer is authorized to bind the devil in the name of Jesus Christ (See Luke 10:19). Why remain silent when the forces of darkness keep attacking you?

8. Be sensitive and specific – (See Eph.6:14). Do not beat the air. Do not spray your bullets carelessly. Target the enemy and what he is doing in your life or in your family. Some people bind all the demons in town and end up not dealing with their problem. Direct your weapons to the root of your problem. Call the spirits by name as you pray.

9. Pray in the Spirit – *"Praying always with all prayer and supplication in the Spirit, being watchful to this end with all perseverance and supplication for all the saints" (Eph.6:18).*

Praying in the Spirit is praying in tongues. Praying in the Spirit is very important in warfare. When you pray in the Spirit, the Holy Spirit directs your prayer to the source of the problem. By praying in the Spirit you also give specific instructions to angels concerning your case.

"Likewise the Spirit also helps in our weaknesses. For we do not know what we should pray for as we ought, but the Spirit Himself makes intercession for us with groanings which cannot be uttered. Now He who searches the hearts knows what the mind of the Spirit is, because He makes intercession for the saints according to the will of God" (Rom.8:26-27).

I am very convinced that if Christians were to become more aggressive and offensive in their prayers, we would see many more miracles.

Is it All Prophetic?

Today, the term "Prophetic" means "inspired by the Holy Spirit". This question keeps ringing in my mind: "Is all I see being practiced during prayer in Churches today inspired by the Holy Spirit?" I watched a preacher jumping and pounding on a woman's belly, back and buttocks many times during ministration. At the end she jumped up and shouted that she was healed. The crowd joined her in frenzied celebration. I also watched a pastor who prayed over car fuel and told the church members that he had turned it to fruit juice. I saw church members scrambling to drink it. Some of them said it was sweet. A lot is going on among God's people nowadays and people say it is "Prophetic." And since some people believe that a prophet cannot be questioned, their members just swallow up everything.

Let us examine the case of Prophet Moses in Numbers 20. During the journey of Israel across the wilderness, the people became very thirsty at a place called Kadesh. When Moses cried to God for intervention, the Lord told him to go and speak to a rock for water to flow out of it. Moses went on and struck the rock twice. Even though he did it his own way, God still honored His word and caused the water to flow out. Now listen to what God said to Moses after the miracle had been done.

"Because you did not believe Me, to hallow Me in the eyes of the children of Israel, therefore you shall not bring this assembly into the land which I have given them" (Num.20:12).
God responded to the action of the man of God but punished him for not honoring Him (God).

We can learn three lessons from this story: First, not everything we call "Prophetic actions" or "the prophetic" is actually inspired by the Holy Spirit. You will agree with me that it was not the Holy Spirit who inspired Moses to strike the rock twice when God had told him to simply speak to it. It was either Moses' spirit or the devil. Second, the fact that it produces results does not mean that God approves of it. The water came out and the people drank but God was not happy with Moses. Third, God can use someone and then later punish them (See Mat.7:21-22). Moses demonstrated great power but could not inherit the Promised Land. Not all that is being done today in the name of the Lord is Prophetic (Inspired by the Holy Spirit). Some of the practices we call "Prophetic" are actually demonic or carnal. This is the reason why we must all watch out against demonic delusions in our times.

Chapter 5

LEARN TO DIAGNOSE THE CAUSE OF YOUR SPIRITUAL PROBLEMS

This chapter is designed to help you identify the probable causes of the spiritual problems your family is facing before you start to pray. It is said that a problem diagnosed is a problem half-solved. I believe that the Holy Spirit will help you to discover what you are supposed to know concerning your case as you determine to know the truth. It was through reading and researching that Daniel understood that there was a time limit to the captivity of Israel.

"In the first year of his reign I, Daniel, understood by the books the number of the years specified by the word of the LORD through Jeremiah the prophet, that He would accomplish seventy years in the desolations of Jerusalem" (Dan. 9: 2).

Ignorance is the greatest tool Satan is using to torment and maintain God's people in bondages. So do not take things for granted; take your time and dig out issues concerning your life and family. Some people live under deception, thinking that all is well when they are actually bound. In June 2011, I was invited to run a Prayer Storm program in a Church in Yaoundé. On the fourth day of the program a lady came up to testify that when her pastor announced the program, she had said it did not concern her since she had been a believer for long. It does not really matter for how long you have been a believer; if you have not dealt with the grip of the enemy over your life, you will still be in bondage. She said that when she came to the service on the third day, I asked that all those who were in the hall should aggressively pray all the prayers even if they did not believe what they were praying. She joined in the prayers and before long she began manifesting strangely. For more than one hour she vomited continually. At the end of the service she felt liberated and was able to sleep very peacefully. It is terrible to feel that you have no problem when the enemy is actually ruining you inside.

Some Symptoms of Evil Foundations

Carefully examine the points below alongside the questions, to find out what the root of the problems your family is facing is. Take time to answer the questions. It is a serious and costly job. You may have to pray and think hard. You may also have to meet with some people to ask questions concerning your family. You may have to read other books for a deeper understanding. Please do not hesitate to invest some money and time into your destiny.

Also remember that symptoms are different from real problems. The symptoms of malaria are: headaches, joint pains, vomiting, high temperature and shivering. But the malaria itself is a parasite that lives in the blood. If you only treat the symptoms, the patient can never be completely free from malaria. That is why Paracetamol is not a drug to treat malaria because it only deals with symptoms like high temperature and pains. Often what we call problems are symptoms. As the Holy Spirit shall help us we want to use the symptoms to track down our problems to the roots. By the time you are through with the root causes of your problems, you will lay a new foundation for the next generation. People with evil foundations have the following symptoms:

Individuals:

1. The person suffers constantly from mental or emotional breakdown.
2. Repeated or chronic sickness, which may be hereditary, with no relief from medical help
3. Sexual harassment in dreams
4. Immoral life (prostitution, rape, pornography, incest and abuse)
5. An irresponsible life style (indebtedness, drugs, drunkenness, gambling)
6. Nightmares and fighting in dreams (spirit husband or wife)
7. Prolonged barrenness and constant threats of miscarriage
8. Breakdown of marriage and family (constant divorce and remarriage, multiple partners)
9. Family misunderstandings

10. Inability to marry
11. Continuous financial insufficiency, despite serious efforts
12. Being accident prone. Falling and rising in the faith
13. Hearing of strange voices and seeing strange apparitions
14. Violence (warlike people)
15. Adamant rejection of the gospel
16. A cruel and wicked character
17. Constantly eating in dreams
18. Constantly fellowshipping with dead people in dreams

Family:

1. Family members suffer constantly from mental or emotional breakdown.
2. Repeated or chronic sicknesses that are common among family members sometimes or often resistant to medical help.
3. Immoral life (prostitution, rape, pornography, incest and abuse) common among family members.
4. Most family members are irresponsible (indebtedness, drugs, drunkenness, gambling).
5. Prolonged barrenness with different family members.
6. Marriages of family members easily breakdown (constant divorce and remarriage, multiple partners).
7. Family misunderstandings very common.
8. Family members find it difficult to marry.
9. Family members work hard but earn very little.
10. Family members are accident prone.
11. Inability to start and finish (school dropout, always starting something new).
12. Limitations in life (financially, spiritually, professionally etc.).

13. Family incidents of untimely death, suicides etc. Read Deuteronomy 28.

Write Down Answers To These Questions
(Use a notebook)

1. What is your family name? ....
2. What is its meaning?...
3. Who gave the name?..
4. Why did they give that name?..
5. Is it the name of a certain person, idol, animal, tree, etc.?..
6. Has any of you in the family been dedicated to a god, a shrine or the palace? ... (If yes, deal with the covenants and destroy any connection you have with them)
7. What is the name of the idol or shrine? ....
8. What are your family idols? Name them; ....
(You have to renounce them, break any covenant with them and also break their influences on your life)
9. Does your family have altars for the worship of ancestors? (skulls, stones, bones, etc.) .... *(If yes you must denounce them. All the objects must be burnt. If you cannot handle them call a deliverance minister)*
10. Do you have a family shrine?.................... (These shrines must be dealt with. I will show you what to do later)
11. What happens there?..
    (You need to know what is done there so as know how to pray and liberate those who are bound by those idols)
12. Who is the priest of that god? ....
13. Who is his next of kin? ....
    (The priest of such idols needs to be delivered)
14. Are there some hills, stones, trees, foods, streams, forests,

markets etc. sacred to your family? ..... There are always spirits associated to such things *(you have to renounce each one of them and declare your total submission to Jesus Christ)*.

15. Is your family house or land located on or near idols, disputed land or ancestral graves? Generally such families are haunted or cursed. You must identify why there are disputes or whether there are any covenants or altars established on the land and deal with them ....

16. Does your family keep traditional objects of worship (juju) or altars? ....

(If yes then you must renounce every covenant your ancestors made with the spirit behind the juju. Mention their names. If the juju is under your power, it should be burnt according to Deuteronomy 7:2, 5; 12:3).

17. What were the occupations of your parents and ancestors?

Father's family..

Mother's family ....

(Sometimes the curses people are suffering from come from the type of occupations their parents were involved in. The occupations of your ancestors can bring a blessing or a curse on your family. Renounce their evil ways Ezekiel 18:1ff. Research has shown that evil occupations of parents lay an evil foundation for the pains of their offspring. Slave traders, traffickers, gamblers, prostitutes, native doctors, thieves, bar owners, corrupt people who receive bribes etc. their children often suffer misery and calamities. You have to cry out for mercy).

18. How did your parents/ grand parents live their marital lives? Father's side: ....

Mother's side ....

(Some got married, divorced and remarried a number of times. That is

a sure evil foundation for unstable marriages. Deal with it severely and be determined to marry in God's will)

19. Are you from a polygamous family? ....

(If yes, deal with the spirit of polygamy. Polygamy is pure rebellion against divine order and it is a terrible sin. It is a breeding ground for family conflicts; see Jacob and David. Deal with the curse of unfaithfulness and multiple partners. Usually children of polygamist have the habit of multiplying partners)

20. If you are from a polygamous family; how does your mother treat the other woman/ women and her/their children? ....

(Some spiritual problems come because of the tears of oppression that are flowing in the polygamous family. Some children and some wives cry day and night because of pains inflicted on them either by the husband or co-wives, etc.).

21. How were the marriages of your parents & grandparents? .... Identify their wrong practices ...... Identify good practices you should copy.............................

23. What disease killed your parents? ....

24. Is there any disease(s) common amongst members of your family? ....

(If yes, then you have to pray hard to cancel the power of that generational disease. Do not conclude that "it is our family sickness". Begin to pray against it so that it will not short-circuit your destiny. My grandmother died of a bronchial problem at the age of 45. My mother began suffering from severe bronchial disorder before she was 40. She believed that she would die before 45. When it was found out that it was a generational problem connected to a curse of pre-mature death she went through deliverance and today she is above 60 years and the problem is nowhere to be found.)

25. Are there some recurrent problems in your family right now? (Joblessness, serious quarrels, etc.)… name them…

26. Are there some particular sins that are common among your family members, so much that people can use them to describe your family? (Stealing, immorality, wickedness, pride, trickery, drunkenness, violence etc.)…

(If yes, deal with the yoke of collective captivity over your life. Watch over your life to ensure that you do not follow the example of your parents and other family members)

27. Did any of your ancestors take a title in the village? …

(If yes you have to deal with the forces behind such offices)

28. Was any of your parents/ancestors part of any cult or secret society?… Which one?… *(If yes, deal with the spirits of those cults laying claim on your lives because of the evil covenants)*

29. Are you a successor?.. to who… Where you initiated?…. Have you been pouring libation to your ancestors?….....

(If yes, deal with ancestral/ familiar spirits and curses. Renounce them and burn down all their altars. You can still be a family head but never pour out libation to any ancestor)

30. Do you as a family or an individual keep any sacred objects? … *(A bag, clay pot, a ring for protection, bangles, a chain, altars raised in your house, candles for prayers, incenses, herbs to burn, tree backs, mirrors, talisman, anointed garments, or anything used for protection and luck. If yes, you must destroy them or take them to any servant of God. If you cannot handle it invite an anointed minister of the gospel of Jesus Christ to help you out)*

31. Have you noticed any abnormality with the progress of your family members? …. (There are heights in life that they can never reach. I met a young girl from a very big family and she told me that none of her family members have ever had the G.C.E Ordinary Level).

Check your financial situation

32. Do you owe people money?...

33. Do you have a problem paying back debts even when you have money? ....…… (If yes, you are bound and need to cry out to God to liberate you)

34. Do you work very hard but earn very little?......................
(If yes, there is a curse of hardship and fruitless labour)

35. Do people owe you and never want to pay back?.............
(If yes, your finances are under satanic attack)

36. Do you have problems paying tithes to God?...................
(If yes, you are under a curse. Repent and be liberated for a season of refreshing to come your way. See Malachi 3:8-12)

37. Do you gladly support the work of God financially? ....
(If not, you cannot enjoy real financial prosperity.)

38. Do you give generously to the needy?................................

39. Do you sow freely into the lives of servants of God?.......

40. Do people easily give to you?................... (If not, then check how much you give out monthly. Your giving will determine your receiving. See Luke 6:38)

41. Do you support your family financially without pressure from your spouse?..

42. Do members of your family succeed in life easily? ....

43. Do you use fake certificates?........ *(If yes, you must deal with that false foundation. Some use other people's certificates to work, some have changed their ages. It is horrible when you who know the truth go that way. You can never reach your best by such methods)*

44. Have you ever used charms to gain favor or a job or to make money?..................… *(If yes, you must deal with the evil covenant with the serpent called Mammon)*

45. Do you have any charm or juju in your business place or a particular law you must keep in order to prosper? ....

(If yes, you need to deal with evil covenants with demons)

46. Have you ever given your money to any shrine, thrown it into a river, a grave, etc.? …......................... *(If yes, then deal with evil covenants with demonic wasters.)*

Check your sexuality

47. Do you fall into sexual immorality often? …....................…
(If yes deal with the any spirit spouse/ and soul ties. See Power Must Change Hands Vol.2)

48. Do you make love with unknown people in your dreams?... how often?.. *(If yes, then you need to deal with spirit wife/ husband and also the influences of evil altars on your life)*

49. Have you made a blood pact with someone before for any reason? …........... *(If yes, you have to deal with soul ties. Renounce that person from your life. Use the blood of Jesus to cancel the evil covenant. Deal with all evil spirits reinforcing that covenant in your life)*

50. Are you divorced? …………………………………………...
(If yes you have to deal with soul ties to completely separate from the person. See Power Must Change Hands Vol.2)

51. Are family members involved with incest? (That is sexual intercourse with relatives: father, sister, brother, mother, cousin, aunt, etc. Any sexual activity with family members brings serious curses on you). *If yes you must deal with the spirit of incest and also with the curse. See Leviticus 18.)*

52. Are family members involved in any same sex relationships; homosexuality or lesbianism? ……............. *(If yes, you must deal with the covenant and the curse)*

62. Did your parents kill people?............. *(If yes, deal with the curse of blood)*

Do a summary

(This is what you are going to use to pray)

After answering all the questions above, use this second section to identify the areas you have to focus your prayers on. As I said earlier, it is serious work. You must take your time if you want to see real results. I dealt with these issues in my life and my family in the days of ignorance. I did not have a prayer book like this one to guide me. By the grace of God today you have a lot of materials. Why not take time to handle these issues that concern you and your family?

"Therefore, brethren, be even more diligent to make your call and election sure, for if you do these things you will never stumble" (2Pet.1:10).

1. Identify the sins you have to confess.
Do this from the questions you have answered above............

2. Name the idols, shrines, and gods you have identified. These are the idols representing the spiritual forces attacking your family. ....

3. Identify the different spirits you must deal with.
 (These are the spirits behind the idols that are re-enforcing curses and problems in your family)...........................

4. Note down the different covenants you have to renounce.
(Personal covenants, family covenants and tribal covenants. See Power Must Change Hands Vol.2&3 for more information on covenants) ....

5. Identify the different areas of curses operating on you and your family. (These are the curses you will beak as you begin to pray) ....

6. Are there some things that must be burnt? Name them.. (You cannot fool God or the demons that are attacking you. It is very strange that today people keep charms, juju, talismans, occult books, horoscope books, etc. and then go around looking for men of God to pray for and deliver them. If you continue like that God will judge you. It is a mockery to God. Surrender those things for destruction before you start praying. If you go on to pray the prayers in this book without destroying all satanic property in your keeping the demons can harm you very badly).

7. Are there some people you or your family must make peace with? Name them .... (Make peace with God and man before you start to pray. Some people have failed to see break through because they have enemies they have refused to forgive. Jesus warned that we should settle our disputes before we come to pray; Matt.5:23-24; 1Pet.3:7).

8. What practical step will you take for reconciliation as an individual and as a family? Write it down...................

9. Are there things or money you owe someone or God as an individual or as a family?. ... What are you going to do to solve it? Write it down...

Note: *Your prayers can never manipulate God to compromise His word. Many people pray and fast a lot but see very few results because they fail to put things in order first. They pray but leave out some practical things they need to do. Sometimes just paying your debt brings breakthrough. Sometimes reconciliation alone brings healing. Be wise.*

Chapter 6

HOW TO CRUSH THE POWERS OF EVIL FORCES

The Bible truth is that you can be totally free from any spiritual bondage you are in now either as an individual or as a family. You can actually come out of that condition and begin to experience abundant life in Jesus Christ. But for your freedom to become a reality two important things are involved: there is WHAT YOU MUST KNOW and WHAT YOU MUST DO. First, you must know what Jesus Christ has done for you on the cross. Second, you must practically apply this knowledge to your situation as I will show you how below. It is only through this that your freedom will become unstoppable.

What I am dealing with here is the core of this book. It is only on the basis of what I am about to explain that you can boldly stand against the kingdom of darkness. Never forget that spiritual warfare is primarily a legal battle. You cannot prevail against the devil and his forces without first securing a legal ground. The legal ground summarily is the price Jesus Christ paid for your freedom on the cross. Anyone trying to do spiritual battle without first securing this legal ground, cannot achieve the expected results. You could even end up a casualty.

Understand Your Freedom in Christ
(What you must know)

1. Jesus Christ died for you
"But God demonstrates His own love toward us, in that while we were still sinners, Christ died for us" (Rom.5:8).
This means that you are free from the death sentence that is supposed to be pronounced on you because of your sins and those you inherited from your ancestors. The power of premature death and the second death is cancelled over you.

2. All your sins have been forgiven
"I write to you, little children, Because your sins are forgiven you for His name's sake" (1Jn.2:12).
You must know with certainty that any sin you have confessed to God, and have abandoned, is forgiven. If your sins have been forgiven, then Satan has lost every legal ground to torment you. Satan has the right to torment only those who live in sin (1Jn.3:38).

3. You have been redeemed

"knowing that you were not redeemed with corruptible things, like silver or gold, from your aimless conduct received by tradition from your fathers, but with the precious blood of Christ, as of a lamb without blemish and without spot" (1Pet.1:18-19).

The word "Redeemed" here means to buy back from the slave market. You were sold to sin and to the devil. You also inherited an evil foundation [curses and evil covenants] from your family. This is what the Bible describes in 1Peter 1:18 as, "*Your aimless conduct received by tradition from your fathers.*" Jesus Christ bought you from the slave market of sin and condemnation with His blood on the cross. You must know without any iota of doubt that you have been bought. You are no longer in the market. If you have been bought from the slave market and released then Satan has lost the right to maintain you in any form of slavery.

4. You have a new citizenship

"For our citizenship is in heaven, from which we also eagerly wait for the Savior, the Lord Jesus Christ" (Phip.3:20).

When you accept Jesus Christ as your Lord and Savior, you are automatically transferred spiritually from the kingdom of darkness to the kingdom of light (Col.1:12-13). You become a child of God (Jn.1:12). The evil foundations laid by your family and tribe no longer have any legal power over because you belong to a new family line called the "Abrahamic family line." Abraham was a blessed man. The Bible in Galatians 3:13-14, 29 reveals that by accepting Jesus Christ as you Savior and Lord you have inherited the same blessings

Abraham received from God. You have to renounce and resist the curses of your old family line and begin to claim the blessings of your new family line.

5. Understand the extent of your redemption
"And they sang a new song, saying: "You are worthy to take the scroll, And to open its seals; For You were slain, And have redeemed us to God by Your blood Out of every tribe and tongue and people and nation" (Rev.5:9).

You must know that Jesus Christ has paid a price to buy you from the ownership of your tribe, tongue, people and nation. Whatever curse is operating on the people of your family or tribe no longer has power over you because you now belong to Jesus Christ. In the physical, I am a Bamumbu man but spiritually, I am a citizen of heaven and not a Bamumbu man. Any curse or set back that is normally supposed to stop any Bamumbu man can no longer stop me because I have been bought and transferred to a new kingdom and tribe; the kingdom of Jesus. If the devil and his demons come around to hinder me, the blood of Jesus will speak on my behalf, telling them that, "Godson has been bought over. He is now a child of God" (Heb.12:24). This is the basis of our spiritual warfare. We want to remind the devil that we are freed by the blood of Jesus Christ and for this reason we must enjoy all He has made available for us: peace, prosperity, good health, eternal life, etc.

6. Satan's claim is cancelled
"Having wiped out the handwriting of requirements that was against us, which was contrary to us. And He

has taken it out of the way, having nailed it to the cross"
(Col.2:14).

Satan has a case file against every sinner. It is this case file that the Bible calls, *"Requirements that was against us."* Jesus Christ took away this case file from Satan and cancelled it with His precious blood. The truth is that if you are a believer, Satan and his demons no longer have any legal grounds to torment you. This explains why you must hate sin and live a holy life. In your spiritual warfare against evil foundations and satanic forces, you are telling the devil that you have been discharged and acquitted so he has no reason to stop you anymore.

Saturate your mind with this revelation and kingdoms will begin to crumble before you as you pray.

Practical Steps to Total Freedom
(What You Must Do)

1. Identify evil foundations
This involves research: Asking questions as seen in chapter 5 and praying to get help from the Holy Spirit.

2. Confess and abandon all evil practices
Confess your sins and those of your ancestors. God is angry when people commit sins (Deut.27:15). Ask God to forgive you because of the death of Christ on the cross for all those sins. Also ask those you have sinned against to forgive you.

3. Renounce (refuse) all evil covenants and pacts
The devil can never bind someone without the provision of an open door. For example, when children are taken to

witchdoctors for protection, these witchdoctors (agents of Satan) establish covenants between them and demons. You have to renounce such covenants.

4. Break the evil foundation

Use the weapons of warfare and aggressively begin to pull down, uproot, scatter and destroy all evil foundations and covenants. Call them by name. At this time do not pray generalized prayers, be specific. See Power Must Change Hands 1. You need the ministration of an anointed servant of God in case you are unable to handle such cases. (Read Deut.33:1; Num.6:22-26).

5. Resist the devil

Satan will not just sit down and see you walk away to liberty. He will fight you with all his strength. That is why when you start to deal with evil foundations, sometimes there are strange reactions and manifestations. If you really want to be free you must fight with all your heart (Mat.11:12), and the evil spirits will flee (Ja.4:7). Some fearful Christians advise that we should leave the devil and his agents alone. Leaving them alone does not make you free from your bondages. If you have discovered a problem in your life, be aggressive and fight your way to freedom, in Jesus' name.

6. Destroy Satan's property

If there is any of his property in your possession, burn it (Acts 19:19-20). This property may be a clay pot, a "country bag", a ring, a charm, occult books, candles, holy water, strange oils, etc. If you continue to keep them, you can never be totally free. In case you are afraid, get the help of an anointed servant of God.

7. Change your beliefs

Reject every wrong belief and accept the word of God as the only guide for your life. Stop interpreting life's situations by the superstitions of your tribe. It may be that in your village, when someone sees a snake around the house it is considered an indication that evil spirits are around. You must renew your mind with the word of God (See Rom.12:1-3). Know that in Christ you have been given power to smash snakes underfoot (See Luke 10:19). As you use the word of God to direct every area of your life, you will continue to enjoy your freedom in Christ. Whenever you decide to keep aside the word of God, Satan and your sinful desires will take you back into captivity.

8. Change your way of life

If you continue in the evil practices of your ancestors, you can never be free. Now that you know the evil they did, choose to act differently. Avoid what destroyed them. This is the only way to rebuild a new foundation. Be very prayerful. Pray strategically (Read my book, *A Dynamic Prayer Life*).

9. Give yourself to reading and mediating on the word

Obey every word to the letter. It is the word of God that will build a new foundation for your life and family. Today you are suffering because your ancestors did not build your family line on the principles of the Bible. Through your dedication to God's word, you have the opportunity to lay a good foundation for those who will be born after now.

10. Give sacrificially

All those who had good spiritual foundations in the Bible were givers. You too must learn to be a sacrificial giver. Do not allow the work of God to suffer disgrace when you are there. When you open up what you have for God's work, He too will make available all He has for you (See Prov.11:24-26).

11. Work hard and smart

God will only bless the works of your hands (See Deut.28:8). He does not release divine blessings into the air. Divine blessings have conditions you must fulfill; smart work is one of these conditions. While you pray, get yourself doing something that can raise money to take care of yourself and of others.

12. Connect to God-fearing people

God fearing people will help you to live your new life in Christ. You will learn from them how to pray and how to practice the commandments of God. An anointed servant of God over you will determine how far you can go in your walk with God.

Part 2:

PROPHETIC PRAYERS

Chapter 7

PROPHETIC PRAISE AND THANKSGIVING

"But You are holy, Enthroned in the praises of Israel"
(Ps.22:3).

God's presence is guaranteed wherever He is praised in spirit and in truth (Jn.4:34). During this season, learn to forget about your challenges and really praise God. When you thank and praise Him for who He is and for what he has already done for you, He will do for you what He has not yet done. Get ready for a new experience with the Holy Spirit as you pray these prayers.

Before you start to pray the prayers below, sing some songs. These could be choruses or hymns.

Praise and thanksgiving prayers

Father, in the name of Jesus:

1. *I thank you for the salvation of my soul.*
2. *I thank you for planting me by the rivers of water and for causing me to flourish in your courts,*
3. *I thank you for making me to be all that I am today.*
4. *I thank you for planting my feet on the rock that can never fail, and that I am still standing.*
5. *I thank you for baptizing me with the Holy Spirit and for loading me with spiritual gifts.*
6. *I praise you for making me, by your power, unstoppable and unbreakable by.*
7. *I praise you for not permitting the wind that sweeps the wicked to sweep me to destruction.*
8. *I praise you because you know all my ways.*
9. *I praise you because from your throne you laugh at the mischief of my enemies.*
10. *I thank you because you shall give my full inheritance in Christ.*
11. *I thank you for giving me power to break my enemies into pieces.*
12. *I thank you because you are my shield and glory.*
13. *I praise you for raising me up such that my enemies cannot put me down.*
14. *I praise you because my horn is exalted in you.*
15. *I worship you because you are a holy God.*
16. *I worship you because you are my eternal rock of ages.*
17. *I praise you the God of all knowledge because nothing is hidden from you.*
18. *I praise you because you are the God who kills and also makes alive.*

19. *I praise you because you are the God who brings down and also lifts up.*

20. *I praise you because you are the God who makes poor and also makes rich.*

21. *I praise you because you are the God who holds the pillars of the earth.*

22. *I praise you because you guard the feet of your saints continuously.*

23. *I thank you because you hear me when I cry to you*

24. *I praise you because you watch over me when I sleep and when I rise.*

25. *I praise you for you are with me when I go out and when I come in.*

26. *I thank you because you turn my distress to praises.*

27. *I thank you for setting me apart for your glory.*

28. *I thank you for accepting my sacrifices.*

29. *I thank you for putting gladness into my heart and causing me to sing a new song.*

30. *I thank you for causing me to lie down in peace and security.*

31. *I praise you for you are my king and you will hear my voice in the morning.*

32. *I praise you because you do not take pleasure in wickedness.*

33. *I thank you for making your way straight before my face.*

34. *Thank you for causing my enemies to fall by their own counsel.*

35. *Thank you for filling my life with abundant joy.*

36. *Thank you for blessing me with unlimited favour.*

37. *I praise you, my physician, who heals me of all my diseases.*

38. *I thank you because you preserve me and none of my bones is broken.*

39. *I thank you because you frustrate the schemes of my enemies and bring them to shame.*

40. *I praise you who strengthen my feet to skip over a wall.*

41. *Thank you because you strengthen my hands to dismantle the strongholds of my enemies.*

42. *I praise you because you cause my enemies to fall in the pit they have dug for me.*

43. *I praise you because you cause the troubles my enemies have prepared for me to return upon them.*

44. *I thank you because you have put a new song in my mouth to praise you forever.*

45. *I praise you because you are a righteous judge.*

46. *I thank you because you have terminated destruction in my life by the blood of Jesus.*

47. *I thank you because you lift me up from the gates of death.*

48. *I praise you because you can never forget the needy.*

49. *I praise you because you break the hand of the wicked and deliver the innocent.*

50. *I praise you because you are king forever.*

51. *I thank you for giving me the desires of my heart.*

52. *I praise you because your word cannot fail in my life.*

53. *I praise you because my enemies will not be exalted over me.*

54. *I thank you because you will not allow me to sleep the sleep of death.*

55. *I thank you because you will enlighten my eyes with the light of your word.*

56. *Thank you for you will not allow my enemies to rejoice over me.*

57. *Thank you for your abundant grace in my life.*

58. *Thank you for turning around my captivity.*

59. *Thank you because you are the portion of my inheritance.*

60. *Thank you because you are my teacher and counselor in the night.*

61. *Thank you because you are at my right hand and I shall not be*

moved.

62. *Thank you because in your presence there is fullness of joy.*

63. *I praise you because you keep me like the apple of your eye.*

64. *I thank you because under the shadow of your wings you keep me from those who hate me and want to destroy me.*

65. *I praise you because you show me your face in righteousness.*

66. *Thank you for giving your angels charge over me.*

67. *66. I thank you because you make me more than a conqueror in Christ Jesus.*

68. *I thank you for turning my curses into blessings.*

69. *I thank you, I thank you, I thank you Father in the name of Jesus. Amen.*

Chapter 8

PROPHETIC DECLARATIONS

Every miracle God operates is tied to His word. Genesis reports that He created the earth by the decrees of His mouth. *"Then God said, 'Let there be light'; and there was light" (Gen.1:3).*Whatever God says is law and cannot be changed. *"The Scripture cannot be broken" (Jn.10:35). "Forever, O LORD, Your word is settled in heaven" (Ps.119:89).*That is why when He intends to bring deliverance and restoration He sends forth His word. The Bible says, *"He sent His word and healed them, And delivered them from their destructions" (Ps.107:20).*

You Shall Declare a Thing
"You will also declare a thing, And it will be established for you; So light will shine on your ways" (Job 22:28).
This verse reveals that you have divine approval to decree the word of God over your life. Whatever thing that agrees with

God's will for your life shall be released for you as you decree it in the name of Jesus Christ.

Death and Life on your Tongue

The Bible reveals that your tongue is a very powerful instrument given to you by God to shape your life.

*"Death and life are in the power of the tongue, And those who love it will eat its fruit" (Prov.18:21).*Your tongue can activate life or death for you. In other words what you say affects your life positively or negatively.

Jesus also taught believers how to deal with their mountains by the power of the tongue.

"For assuredly, I say to you, whoever says to this mountain, 'Be removed and be cast into the sea,' and does not doubt in his heart, but believes that those things he says will be done, he will have whatever he says" (Mk.11:23).

If you are a believer, then your tongue is a mountain mover. Take your stand on the finished work of Calvary. Remind yourself of your Sonship in Christ Jesus. Buttress your faith on the promises of God. Open your mouth and begin to decree God's word over your life.

Each of these prophetic decrees is drawn from the promises that God has given to us in His word. As you declare them in faith, heaven will establish them for you. Spiritual power will be activated around your life for your transformation, deliverance, healing, restoration and breakthrough. Angels will be released to cause your word for this season to come to pass.

Prophetic Decrees

1. *Through the mercy of the Most High God I decree that I shall not be moved in Jesus' name.*

2. *I decree that from this day, my light will continue to shine from glory to glory, in Jesus' name.*

3. *I declare that in this season my hand shall be stronger than that of my enemies, in the name of Jesus.*

4. *From this month I decree that the goodness and mercy of God shall follow me everywhere I go in Jesus' name.*

5. *I declare that, my testimony shall turn the nations to the Lord in the name of Jesus.*

6. *I declare that the children the Lord has given me shall serve Him in their generation in Jesus' name.*

7. *From today, my own portion of the good of this land is opened up to me in the name of Jesus.*

8. *By the power of the resurrection of our Lord Jesus Christ, I speak life to dead things in my life, in the name of Jesus.*

9. *By the power of the resurrection of our Lord Jesus Christ, let me be catapulted to the level my enemies say I will never reach, in the name of Jesus.*

10. *I declare that I shall have unstoppable advancement from today in Jesus' Name.*

11. *I declare that this year, treasures of dark places shall be transferred to my bosom, in Jesus' Name.*

12. *I declare that this year, my star shall arise and shall fall no more, in Jesus' Name.*

13. *I decree that this year, men shall chase me around with blessings, in Jesus Name.*

14. *I recover ten-fold all my wasted years, in Jesus' Name.*

15. *I decree that this year, men shall compete to favor me, in Jesus' Name*

16. *The works of my hands shall be favored in the name of Jesus.*

17. *I declare that all the days of my life, I shall be a wonder to unbelievers in the name of Jesus.*

18. *I declare that it shall be well with me, my family, my church and my nation in the name of Jesus.*

19. *Let doors of promotion and favour, open for me, in the name of Jesus.*

20. *I declare that from this season by the power of the Holy Spirit I am moving from the minimum level of life to the maximum in the name of Jesus.*

21. *Through the mercy of the Most High God I decree that I shall not be moved in Jesus' name.*

22. *I decree that from this day, my light will continue to shine from glory to glory, in Jesus' name.*

23. *I declare that in this season my hand shall be stronger than that of my enemies, in the name of Jesus.*

24. *From this month I decree that the goodness and mercy of God shall follow me everywhere I go in Jesus' name.*

25. *I declare that, my testimony shall turn the nations to the Lord in the name of Jesus.*

26. *I declare that the children the Lord has given me shall serve I decree that the light of God shall never go out of my family in   the name of Jesus.*

27. *I declare open every closed door in my life in Jesus' name.*

28. *I declare that by the mercy of God, every scarcity in my life is turning to abundance in Jesus' name.*

29. *From today no devil shall put a yoke on me again in Jesus' name.*

30. *In the mighty name of Jesus the power of God shall always shield me and overshadow me.*

31. *In the mighty name of Jesus, I shall fulfill my divine destiny.*

32. *In the mighty name of Jesus, I shall leave a legacy for my descendants.*

33. *I shall not die before my time in the name of Jesus.*

34. *I shall be an all-round fruitful Christian in the name of Jesus.*

35. *I declare that power must change hands in my life in the name of Jesus.*

Part 3:

PRAYER
MARATHON

Note: Do the Prophetic Thanksgiving Prayers in Chapter 7 before you begin praying every day. Also round up every day with the Prophetic Declarations in Chapter 8.

DAY 1

A DIVINE BATH

"Let us draw near with a true heart in full assurance of faith, having our hearts sprinkled from an evil conscience and our bodies washed with pure water" *(Heb.10:22).*

During the next 30 days we want to encounter God in a very special way. I believe that just as he spoke to me in December last year promising that in 2015 He is beginning a great work of restoration in families, His power will rain down on us daily as we spend this one month on this Mountain of Restoration.

The encounter with God's anointing of restoration can only take place on holy ground. This is the reason why we have to start this one month of prayer by consciously consecrating ourselves entirely to the Lord. Consecration is the first step in the journey of effective prayer (Jam.5:16). When Moses met with God at Mount Horeb, He told him, *"Take your sandals off your feet, for the place where you stand is holy ground" (Ex.3:5).*

God wanted Moses to understand from the onset that the only ground upon which He relates with man is HOLINESS. It is in the same vein that Peter speaks to us in 1Peter 1:15-16, *"but as He who called you is holy, you also be holy in all your conduct, because it is written, "Be holy, for I am holy."*

David too understood the implication of trying to seek God with sin in one's life and he said, *"If I had ignored my sins,*

the Lord would not have listened to me" (Ps.66:18) GNT.

Beloved, today is a day of consecration. There are three things that have to be done:

1. Repent of your sins and surrender your life to Jesus Christ

Do it now if you have not yet done so. If you have not yet surrendered your life to Jesus Christ then you do not have the license to pray in His name. Attempting to fast and pray in the name of Jesus without first of all surrendering your whole life to him is mere waste of time.

The Bible promises that God will forgive you and give you new life if you repent from your sins and accept Jesus Christ as your personal Lord and Savior.

"If we say that we have no sin, we deceive ourselves, and the truth is not in us. If we confess our sins, He is faithful and just to forgive us our sins and to cleanse us from all unrighteousness" (1Jn1:8-9).

"But as many as received Him, to them He gave the right to become children of God, to those who believe in His name" (Jn.1:12).

How can you receive Jesus Christ as your Savior and Lord? It is simple! Kneel down now and pray this prayer from your heart:

"Dear Lord Jesus Christ, I need you now. I open the door of my life and receive you as my Savior and Lord. I repent of all my sins now.

Forgive me and wash me with your blood. Make me the kind of person you want me to be from today. Thank you for saving me. Amen!"

Congrats! You are now a child of God. Call me right now let me pray for you: (+237.674.495.895 or 699.902.618). Send me an SMS or an email through: voiceofrevivalcameroon@yahoo.com

2. Let the backslider return to the Lord

A backslider is a believer who used to be a dedicated follower of Jesus Christ but who turned away from the Lord and is presently living in sin. In case you are a backslider, God is calling you today to return to Him for your restoration. It doesn't matter how the devil has messed you up, the Lord will clean you up and clothe you with His glory again. The Bible says there is hope for you because you are still alive.

"Return to the stronghold, You prisoners of hope. Even today I declare That I will restore double to you" (Zec.9:12).
"Return, backsliding Israel,' says the LORD; 'I will not cause My anger to fall on you. For I am merciful,' says the LORD; 'I will not remain angry forever" (Jer.3:14).

Somebody called me one day and said, "Pastor, I have been a backslider for ten years, can God accept me back? If yes, what should I do?" I responded with excitement, "Yes, you can come back right now. Go on your knees and ask Jesus to forgive all your sins. Ask Him to come back into your heart." Dear friend, if you are in a similar situation, kneel down now and pray that God will forgive you and give you a second chance. Stand on the two scriptures above and claim your restoration.

3. Child of God consecrate your life to the Lord

Even as a believer, you have to set your heart in order for God's glory to explode in your life in this season. Pray and ask the Holy Spirit to search and expose to you any evil that may be hidden in your heart and which you do not know about. Pray like David;

"Search me, O God, and know my heart: try me, and know my thoughts: And see if there be any wicked way in me, and lead me in the way everlasting." (Ps.139:23-24).

One other thing about your heart is that it can be attacked by the spirit of distraction and confusion. You need grace to be focused on God as you spend time before Him on this mountain. During this season of prayer the Lord is saying emphatically,

"Pray to Me, and I will listen to you. And you will seek Me and find Me, when you search for Me with all your heart." (Jer.29: 12-13).

I therefore encourage you to seek God with all your heart. Refuse to let anything cheat you by distracting you.

PRAYER POINTS

1. *Examine your life and confess to God any sin and negligence you are convicted of.*
2. *My Father, My Father, give me a divine bath by the blood of Jesus, in Jesus' name.*
3. *Dear Holy Spirit, expose to me any sin that can act as a setback to my prayers during this season of prayer.*

4. *I receive divine cleansing in my spiritual eyes, ears and my mind by the fire of the Holy Ghost, in Jesus name.*

5. *I receive total purification by the precious blood of Jesus Christ now, in the name of Jesus.*

6. *Lord, I dedicate my life and the lives of all those who are involved in this annual fast to your grace, in the name of Jesus. (Mention the organs of your body as well as your soul and spirit).*

7. *Father, I dedicate this fasting month entirely to you, in the name of Jesus Christ.*

8. *O Lord, don't allow the devil and his agents to cheat me of one second, in the name of Jesus.*

9. *Lord, anoint my ears to hear you better and my eyes to see your glory in the name of Jesus.*

10. *O Lord, fill me with the spirit of brokenness and holiness as I seek you this season, in Jesus' name.*

11. *Lord, give me a pure heart and fill me with the fear of God, in Jesus' name.*

12. *Let every filthy garment in my life burn to ashes in Jesus' name.*

13. *Let every power of defilement that has been polluting my life receive fire, in Jesus' name.*

14. *I bind and overpower every anti-holiness spirit operating in my life, in Jesus' name.*

15. *I receive the garment of holiness over my life, in Jesus' name.*

16. *I receive the garment of fire, in Jesus' name.*

17. *I welcome the anointing on my spiritual eyes, ears, and senses.*

18. *O Lord, baptize me and all those praying this season with the anointing of fervent and effective prayer, in Jesus' name.*

19. *Let every hidden secret I am supposed to know concerning my destiny be exposed this month, in Jesus' name.*

20. *I bind and cast away any demonic power assigned to defile and frustrate my prayer during this fast, in the mighty name of Jesus.*

21. *O Lord, help me to put away from my life anything that makes me blemished before your face, in the name of Jesus.*

22. *Lay your hand on your head and pray, "I receive the anointing for total restoration, now, In Jesus' name!."*

23. *O Lord, have mercy on my family and open the door of grace for us this season, in Jesus' name.*

24. *Present each member of your family to God and ask God to visit them with salvation, healing, deliverance and restoration this month.*

DAY 2

LET YOUR GATES OPEN

"Lift up your heads, O you gates! And be lifted up, you everlasting doors! And the King of glory shall come in. Who is this King of glory? The LORD strong and mighty, The LORD mighty in battle" (Ps.24:7-8).

There are some spiritual doors that must open to you in this season for God's ordained blessings to manifest in your life. Today, I want us to labor in prayer to ensure that these doors are opened to us.

Bible scholars say that the gates and doors David is referring to in Psalm 24:7-8, are the gates and doors of the temple in Jerusalem. King David got this revelation as he watched the priest enter the temple with the Ark of the Covenant which represented the presence of God. He saw God's glory invading the temple as the king entered it triumphantly. This king is Jesus Christ (The Messiah), who is the King of kings and the Lord of lords, who is also called the King or Lord of Glory (1Cor.2:8; Ja.2:1).

As these gates and doors we are going to deal with open up in your life, the glory of God shall invade your life and family. Psalm 24:8 says that this King of Glory who is coming into your life and family is, **"The LORD strong and mighty, The LORD mighty in battle."** Wherever He reigns, He puts His enemies under His feet (1Cor.15:25). It is this King of Glory, the Lord mighty in battle who will subdue the powers of darkness and bring perfect restoration into your life and family in this season. Your part is to ensure that the gates and doors are opened.

1. The Door of Grace

We can receive from God only by grace and never by merit. It is for this reason that you should cry to God and say, "Lord, as I come to you on this mountain, open the 'Door of grace' for me by your mercy." The Bible says,

"Let us therefore come boldly to the throne of grace, that we may obtain mercy and find grace to help in time of need" (Heb.4:16).

There is a level of grace needed to deal with every challenge you are facing. The New Living Translation says,

"...There we will receive his mercy, and find grace to help us when we need it most."

This is the time when you need the grace of God most. May the door of grace for total restoration open for you and your family, in Jesus' name.

2. The Door Prayer

There is an anointing that comes on a person or a people to enable the birthing of destinies. For this anointing to come on us, the door of prayer must open to us. When the door of prayer is opened, there is grace released to pray and to see results.

"Before she was in labor, she gave birth; Before her pain came, She delivered a male child. Who has heard such a thing? Who has seen such things? Shall the earth be made to give birth in one day? Or shall a nation be born at once? For as soon as Zion was in labor, She gave birth to her children" (Isa.66:7-8).

It is not by your own strength that you are going to pray and turn around the captivity of your family. You need a supernatural dimension. The Lord will do it for you. He is releasing fresh fire on His people to enable them pray their way to breakthrough. Ask for this anointing for total recovery to come on you.

3. The Door of Revelation

The door of revelation opens to usher in the anointing of wisdom and revelation. (Eph.1:15-16). It is by this anointing that we can understand and walk in the ways of God. This anointing gives us access into the deep things of God, exposing to us His standards, His requirements and the riches of His glory. By this anointing God will tear apart veils and cause you to lay hold of the root causes of some problems you are facing, and the keys to help you solve them. As this door of revelation opens to you, Jesus Christ who is the Lord of lords and King of kings will break open every seal and mystery that has kept your life and family in bondage.

"But one of the elders said to me, 'Do not weep. Behold, the Lion of the tribe of Judah, the Root of David, has prevailed to open the scroll and to loose its seven seals" *(Rev.5:5).*

Stop weeping, and ask the Lord to open the door of revelation for you. There are things you must know in order to enhance your restoration. Receive the grace to know them, in Jesus' name.

4. The Door of Faith

When the door of faith opens, great miracles begin to happen. This is because when this door opens the Spirit of faith is released, and empowers people to believe God for great things. Apostle Paul experienced this in his ministry

"Now when they had come and gathered the church together, they reported all that God had done with them, and that He had opened the door of faith to the Gentiles" (Acts 14:27).

Multitudes of Gentile people began to repent from their sins and turn to Jesus Christ when the door of faith was opened. We need this door to open for miracles of salvation, healing, deliverance and restoration to begin to manifest in our lives and families.

5. The Door of Power

When the door of power is opened unto you, God's miraculous power that changes situations is made available for you. Jesus told His disciples not to leave Jerusalem until the door of power was opened to them.

"...but tarry in the city of Jerusalem until you are endued with power from on high" (Luke 24:49).

The door of power was opened unto them on the day of Pentecost. From that day, diverse kinds of miracles began to manifest among them. As this door of power is opened unto your family, God's power will work out miraculous transformations and restorations.

6. The Door of Angelic Ministry

When this door is opened, you begin to enjoy angelic ministrations. This door was opened to Jacob after his father blessed him and released him (Gen.28:1).

"Then he dreamed, and behold, a ladder was set up on the earth, and its top reached to heaven; and there

the angels of God were ascending and descending on it" (Gen.28:12).

From that time on, you see angels ministering to Jacob on different occasions.

May this door open for you in this season, in the name of Jesus. Let God's angels come into your family and begin to handle cases that have challenged human all endeavors.

PRAYER POINTS

1. *Father, forgive me and my family for closing our doors with sin (Identify the sins and confess them).*

2. *O Lord, purge me and my family from any sin that closes our spiritual doors, in the name of Jesus.*

3. *Let doors of iniquity that have been opened against us be closed, in Jesus' name.*

4. *Holy Father, release your righteous hand and let anything that seeks to exalt itself above Jesus Christ in my life and my family be overthrown, in the name of Jesus.*

5. *Let the evil reign of sin (immorality, idolatry, wickedness, drunkenness, hatred, witchcraft, etc) in my family expire, in the name of Jesus.*

6. *My Father, My Father, arise and let the evil spirits responsible for sin in my life and my family be pulled down forever, in the name of Jesus.*

7. *Lift up your head o you gates, let the King of glory come in and reign in my family.*

8. *O Lord my God, I crown Jesus Christ as the Lord of my life and my family from today.*

9. *My Father, by your mercy, open the door of grace for me and my family this season and let your blessings flow.*

10. *O Lord, let the door of revelation be opened in my life and my family and let the forces of revelation be activated for multiple*

divine revelations in our lives, in the name of Jesus.

11. *O Lord, arise and let every veil, seal or mystery behind our troubles be exposed by your light, in Jesus' name.*

12. *In Jesus' name, I receive grace for uncommon understanding in the things of God.*

13. *In the name of Jesus, I receive divine keys to unlock uncommon doors in my life and my family.*

14. *Father, let the Holy Spirit invade every domain of my life and cause me not to miss any encounter you have ordained for me on this mountain, in the name of Jesus.*

15. *O Lord, clothe me today with the garment of righteousness, in the name of Jesus.*

16. *Lord, oil my life with the anointing that gives access to your presence.*

17. *Go back and pray that each of the doors we have mentioned above will open for you, your family and all those who are participating in this program.*

DAY 3

CLEAN THE HOUSE

"And many who had believed came confessing and telling their deeds. Also, many of those who had practiced magic brought their books together and burned them in the sight of all. And they counted up the value of them, and it totaled fifty thousand pieces of silver" (Acts 19:18-19).

Today, we want to continue to prepare ourselves before we engage in the battle for the restoration of the fortunes of our families. We will do this by carrying out thorough cleaning in our houses. The Lord is commanding us to remove all accursed things from our homes. He wants to establish His presence in the midst of your family and to carry out a deep work of restoration. For this to happen, He says,

"Therefore "Come out from among them And be separate, says the Lord. Do not touch what is unclean, And I will receive you" (2Cor.6:17).

We can learn from this scripture that the pre-requisite for a divine visitation is deliberate separation from that which is unclean before God. This is exactly what the new believers in Ephesus did (Acts 19:14-18). As soon as they received Jesus Christ as their Lord and Savior, they went on to confess their evil deeds publicly and also burnt their occult books and satanic objects that were in their keeping. According to the New Living Translation, the estimated cost of those objects stood at several millions of dollars (Note that one million dollars is about five hundred million francs CFA).

This brings out two truths: First, it is very costly to serve the devil. Imagine the millions these people invested in occultism. Second, those who want to follow Jesus must destroy all satanic objects in their keeping no matter their cost. It is only by doing this that the power for growth and multiplication is released.

"So the word of the Lord grew mightily and prevailed" (Acts 19:20).

Accursed Objects
 An accursed object is a thing that carries a curse. Whoever keeps such a thing accommodates the curse consciously or unconsciously. Check out whether any of the following is in your house. Take action today and remove them:

1. Occult books:
These include sacred books of secret societies like ARMORC, Free Masonry, seven books of Moses, etc.

2. Horoscope books:
Those who follow Horoscope open themselves up to astral spirits. It is the word of God not the stars that should order your destiny.

3. Sacred objects:
There are different types of sacred objects: those that you collected from witch doctors for protection or as charms for love, power or riches. Some sacred objects were handed down to some people by their ancestors. I once prayed for a man who had a certain ugly bangle. He told me it was handed

down to him by his grandmother for his protection.

4. Stolen objects:

Some people have stolen things in their homes. You have to clean them away from your house. One day I went out to pray with a family in Bamenda. While I was still sharing the word of God, the wife of the man who invited me interrupted me. She confessed that she was a thief. She brought down a picture from their wall and told me that twenty years earlier she had stolen the frame from a certain shop in Yaounde. She said that the picture would never hang on her wall again. She showed me an ironing table which she had taken from the sewing workshop of her school. She said, "Pastor, I am a thief this table is not supposed to be in my house. It was bought by the government, to be used for the training of our children. I will take it back to school on Monday." Do you have stolen things in your house? What are things that are supposed to be in the office doing in your house? Clean your house today.

5. God's property:

Things that have been dedicated for the service of God should never become your personal property. When Ananias and his wife Saphira vowed to sell their land and give God the money, they did not understand that through the promise all the money they had received for the land had become God's money. They lost their lives for stealing (Acts5:1-10). Sometimes in Church, money that was contributed for God's work ends up in people's pockets. A pastor told me that he is a child of God so he has the right to eat his father's money. I fear such courage. No one can steal from God and go free.

Check your house to see whether you are keeping anything that is supposed to be in God's house. If yes take it back to His house immediately. If you have eaten God's money, go and confess to the pastor. Also pay back the money.

6. Other people's property:

Some people use ungodly methods to seize property from others. When you bring such things into your family, you attract curses. A man confessed to me not long ago that his father and uncles snatched land by force from some people. He said he is trying to convince his brothers and sisters to return the land to the legitimate owners. This is cleaning the house. People's property you have borrowed and have refused to return can become accursed objects in your house too. For example, people's books you borrowed to read and failed to return them.

7. Anointed objects:

"Anointed objects" from demonic sources are accursed objects. These could include oils, water, candles, crucifixes, pieces of cloth, portraits, stones, etc. Some people don't care about the sources of the "anointed objects", they just carry them. Some of these things have been anointed by the devil to serve as distractors and pollutants.

As far as God is concerned, you must remove these things from your house.

"But thus you shall deal with them: you shall destroy their altars, and break down their sacred pillars, and cut down their wooden images, and burn their carved images with fire" (Deut. 7:5).

When Israel under King Hezekiah cleansed the temple of the

Lord, revival broke out in the land. I assure you; if you will cleanse your house both as an individual and as a family, God's glory will come down.

Allow the Holy Spirit to help you identify these things so that you can deal with them. Unfortunately most people only want to pray. They are not interested in removing pollutants from their lives. If you ignore what I am dealing with here, your prayers will be impotent. Take action immediately!

You may need counseling concerning how to deal with some of these things. Do not hesitate to call us or meet any other anointed servant of God for assistance.

PRAYER POINTS

1. *O Lord, thank you for your anointed word to me today.*
2. *Father, I submit totally to your will and authority, in the name of Jesus.*
3. *I receive grace today to purge my life, my house and my family of all those things that belong to the devil, in Jesus' name.*
4. *Father, in the name of Jesus, I renounce and reject all satanic property in my keeping, in the name of Jesus.*
5. *I renounce any covenant I have established with evil spirits through these demonic objects, in the name of Jesus.*
6. *I cancel every demonic covenant with the blood of Jesus and I declare that I am free by the blood Jesus.*
7. *I bind any evil spirit that has invaded my life, my house and my family because of these satanic objects, in Jesus name.*
8. *As I burn these satanic objects, I declare that their authority over me, my house and my family is broken forever, in Jesus' name.*
9. *Let the fire of the Holy Ghost begin to burn in my life, my house and my family now! In the name of Jesus*

10. *I release myself from all ancestral demonic defilements, in the name of Jesus.*

11. *I release myself from any demonic pollution from my parents' religion, in the name of Jesus.*

12. *I release myself from every demonic pollution coming from my past involvement with any false religion or occult society, in the name of Jesus.*

13. *I release myself from every dream pollution, in the name of Jesus.*

14. *Lay your hand on your stomach and pray violently seven times: "I command every evil plant in my life to come out with its roots, now, In the mighty name of Jesus!."*

15. *I vomit out every demonic food, poison and drink I have taken into my body, in the name of Jesus. Declare it seven times. After declaring fervently seven times, just cough out a few times.*

16. *Let all negative materials circulating in my blood stream be flushed out by the blood of Jesus, in the name of Jesus.*

17. *Let any evil hand that comes to feed me in the dream be roasted by fire, in the name of Jesus.*

18. *Lay you hand on your head and pray aggressively and insistently at least seven times: Let the fire of the Holy Spirit burn in all the organs of my body; my eyes, ears, tongue, intestines, liver, heart, lungs, kidneys, etc. in the mighty name of Jesus.*

19. *I bind and cast out all spirits of defilement assigned against my family, in the name of Jesus.*

20. *Let the fire of the Holy Ghost roast to ashes powers responsible for oppression and diseases in my life, in Jesus' name.*

21. *You foul spirit re-enforcing pollution in my life and family, pack and go, in Jesus' name.*

22. *Yoke of pollution on my life and family, scatter now, In the name of Jesus!*

23. *I declare that from today, my life, my house, and my family are no-go zones for all unclean spirits, in Jesus' name.*
24. *Father, establish your glory over us from today, in Jesus' name.*

DAY 4

O LORD, SEND US REVIVAL

"Will You not revive us again, That Your people may rejoice in You?" (Ps.85:6).

What is "revival"?

Revival is a move of the Holy Spirit among God's people that generates a fresh revelation of the person of Jesus Christ and provokes God's people to return to the ways of God. True spiritual revival is God amongst His people revealing His holiness, mercy and power. Peter C. Wagner says, "An authentic spiritual revival is the result of a deep out pour of the Holy Spirit in the lives of those who have been regenerated by Him according to their faith in Christ as Lord." Spiritual revival is heaven's response to desperate cries of help from God's children. We need revival in the Church to prepare the Church for the rapture.

The Results of Revival

The first mark of a true revival is the restoration of the consciousness of God among His people, which leads to genuine repentance and commitment to live holy lives.

Secondly, there is a demonstration of the power of God through the gifts of the Holy Spirit. The preaching of the word of God is backed by signs and wonders.

Thirdly, there is a mighty harvest of souls into God's kingdom. There is visible qualitative and quantitative Church growth.

When the early Church sought God and His presence was released on them, both their spiritual and physical needs were met. We desperately need God in the Church in this nation today.

The Need for Revival

There is gross spiritual darkness over the nations of the earth. Evil is rising at an alarming rate. We need a greater power to confront these forces. We are facing many challenging problems today that no human effort can resolve. Many false religions are growing very fast nowadays. In some places they are multiplying faster than Christianity. There is an upsurge of satanic activity in our times. That is why we need a revival.

The Church which is supposed to provide an answer to this end time moral decay and spiritual oppression that is so common in our days, is seemingly losing the fire. As someone said, "The Church is becoming very broad but only a few inches deep." People commit sin but are still bold enough to stand and minister before God's people. We have preachers who say that they are not called to preach on sin but on prosperity. The world is becoming churchy, while the church is fast becoming worldly. We need a revival.

There is hope; God is sending a revival in answer to our earnest prayers.

Some Examples from History

Every revival in history came about because someone or some group of Christians fasted and prayed to move the hand of God for revival/harvest.

It is said that Evan Roberts and his group of young

saints fasted and prayed for five years and God moved mightily over Wales, and then the Great Welsh Revival took place. This revival lasted about eighteen months and harvested between 100,000 and 180,000 new converts.

Charles Finney and a group of Christians fasted and prayed for over six years before the Second Reformation was sparked.

William Seymour and Frank Bartleman fasted and prayed for almost seven years before God moved and the Azusa Street Revival was birthed. They were so skinny from fasting that their wives feared for their lives. The Azusa Street Revival brought in huge numbers. The spread of Pentecostalism around the world began from Asuza. Today there are 1 billion Pentecostals in the entire world.

The Price for Revival

Every revival, big or small, was preceded by much fasting and praying put in by some faithful Christians or groups of saints. Until some people become ready to pay the price there will be no revival in the church or in the land.

Daniel in Babylon:

When Daniel, the prophet, learned that Jeremiah had prophesied that Israel would be in slavery in Babylon for seventy years, he set himself to fast and pray for the release of Israel. He knew that the seventy years were almost over (Da.9:2). As a result of Daniel's fasting and prayers, God freed Israel from captivity. Even though it had been prophesied by Jeremiah, Daniel knew that God wanted someone to fast and pray for it to come to pass. God respects our will and so He will not do something on His own or without someone asking Him to. Of course, the more important the movement or event is, the more fasting and praying are required.

The coming of the messiah:

Isaiah and other prophets prophesied often of the coming of the Messiah. In fact, many were looking for the Messiah in the days of Jesus.

Philip found Nathanael and said to him, "We have found Him of whom Moses in the law, and also the prophets, wrote—Jesus of Nazareth, the son of Joseph" (JN.1:45). They knew what the prophets had said about the coming of the Messiah. But, it was not automatic just because Moses and other prophets such as Isaiah had prophesied His coming. God raised Simeon and Anna to fast and pray for many years for the coming of Jesus (Lk.2:25-27). Anna fasted and prayed for over 64 years before Jesus came in the flesh.

Why Much Prayer and Fasting is Needed

Why must we labor in prayer and fasting before revival can break out in our midst.

1. The problem of sin:

The sins and the abominations that have been committed in the land for many generations have caused God to release many curses on the land. These sins have also given the forces of darkness the legal right to oppress people. These sins must be dealt with in serious prayers and fasting before the strongholds of the devil can be dismantled over the land.

Galatians 3:13 says, *"Christ hath redeemed us form the curse of the law, being made a curse for us: for it is written, Cursed is every one that hangeth on a tree:..."* Jesus' sacrifice on the cross made a way for all curses to be broken by His blood, once the sin is forgiven. We must pray for this to become a reality in our lives in the land.

2. Resistance by the devil:

The devil knows that the coming of a revival means the establishment of the reign of Jesus Christ and the termination of his wicked rule. Therefore, he will fight with all his might to stop any revival.

The Bible says that Satan is the prince of the power of the air (Eph.2:2). Even Jesus called him the ruler of this world (Jn.12:1; Jn.14:30; Jn.16:11). He is the prince of the power of the air because he rules from the mid-heavens, the atmosphere around the earth. That is why Jesus said,

". . . whatsoever you shall bind on earth shall be bound in heaven: and whatsoever thou shall loose on earth shall be loosed in heaven" (Mat.16:19; Mt.18:18).

We on earth have to pray and bind up Satan's strong men in the mid-heavens. In fact, unless we bind up Satan's ruling spirits or strong men, they will oppose and block any revival/harvest. Therefore, part of our praying must include binding up of Satan's strong men. Jesus said,

"Or else how can one enter into a strong man's house, and spoil his goods, except he first bind the strong man? and then he will spoil his house" (Mt.12:29).

It is Time to Pray

Prior to every revival, God raises some individuals to

mobilize others to seek Him for the out pour of the Holy Spirit. God expects us to do corporate prayers. This is part of the assignment God has given to us. Christian Restoration Network has the mandate to mobilize God's people to pray for revival in families, churches, our nation and the nations.

"When I shut up heaven and there is no rain, or command the locusts to devour the land, or send pestilence among My people, 'if My people who are called by My name will humble themselves, and pray and seek My face, and turn from their wicked ways, then I will hear from heaven, and will forgive their sin and heal their land" (2Chron.7:14).

God's idea here is "My people." He is not talking about an individual. Everyone has a part to play. If all of us will humble ourselves and seek God at this time of the latter rain, there will be a mighty revival.

Many believers who are conversant with God's prophetic agenda for Cameroon know that there is a mighty spiritual revival that is coming to Cameroon. Read my book, *"Your Time for Divine Expansion: A prophetic Message to the Church in Cameroon."*

In the seventies a man of God called Steve Lightle visited Cameroon from Braunschweig, Germany. He came because during a prayer meeting with a group of believers they had seen a vision of the map of Africa shining. The light source was Cameroon. Many other startling prophecies make it clear that God has a great plan for our nation. This great revival that will shake Cameroon and flow out to other nations will come through labour in prayer. We must sanctify ourselves and begin to seek God. The burden to fast for 30 days every year was born in my heart from this vision of the forth-coming revival in Cameroon. I still believe God for this great revival. I want you to consecrate your life so that God can prepare you to become an instrument in this coming revival.

God will not move His hand until someone or some group fasts and prays for revival. It is a spiritual principle. Similarly, although the Bible reveals that there will be one last and great revival/harvest before the end of the world, God will not move His hand to bring revival unless someone or some group fasts and prays for it. It is important that we begin to fast and pray for revival.

PRAYER POINTS

1. *Lord, thank you for today and for our beloved nation Cameroon. (Take time and worship God for all He has invested in Cameroon and for what He is doing in this nation).*
2. *Plead with God to forgive Cameroon for the sins of corruption, rejection of the gospel, homosexuality, lesbianism, occultism, witchcraft, idol worship, evil traditions, human sacrifice, prostitution, crime, bribery, tribalism, confidence in self, drunkenness, killing, etc.*
3. *Ask God to purify the land with the blood of Jesus.*
4. *Renounce every satanic covenant our leaders have made with occult societies.*
5. *Ask the blood of Jesus to speak on behalf of Cameroon, nullifying every claim Satan holds against us.*
6. *O Lord, release the fire of judgment against all forces of darkness oppressing our leadership.*
7. *O Lord, release your hand against demonic powers oppressing our economy.*

8. *Lord, release the spirit of conviction on the nation of Cameroon.*

9. *Let prison doors of sin open for the salvation of Cameroonians in Jesus' name.*

10. *O Lord, pour your Spirit afresh on the Church in Cameroon.*

11. *O Lord, forgive the Church in Cameroon for being indifferent.*

12. *Lord, forgive the evil and wickedness that is going on in the Churches, hindering unbelievers from changing.*

13. *O Lord, pour out the Spirit of aggressive prayer on all the Christians in every denomination.*

14. *Lord, pour out the Spirit of righteousness and the fear of God on all the Christians.*

15. *O Lord, do a work of sanctification in the Churches.*

16. *Let there be rapid spiritual growth in your Church in Cameroon in Jesus' name.*

17. *O Lord, let the Church grow in number in Jesus' name.*

18. *O Lord, restore unity in the Churches in Jesus' name.*

19. *Lord, cause Christians from different denominations to be united.*

20. *O Lord, release a mighty anointing for signs and wonders in the Churches in Jesus' name.*

21. *We break every veil of religion over the people in Jesus' name.*

22. *Lord, send revival among the Catholics, Moslems, Jehovah witnesses etc.*

23. *O Lord, send grace for financial prosperity in the Churches in Cameroon.*

24. *O Lord, let the Churches not be distracted from the mission of the Church, which is missions.*

25. *Arise O Lord, and let the forces of darkness gathered against the Church in Cameroon be scattered in Jesus' name.*

26. *We pull down every occult power invoked against the Church in Jesus' name.*

27. *We command the heavens to be opened over the Church in*

Cameroon in Jesus' name.

28. O Lord, create a spirit of humility and brokenness among the believers.

29. O Lord, reveal to believers the depth and the evil of their sins in Jesus' name.

30. O Holy Spirit, move on the believers and cause them to confess and repent of their sins.

31. O Lord, grant the believers hunger for your word and a readiness to obey it in Jesus' name.

32. Dear Holy Spirit, stir within every believer a desire to search and to know the Word of God.

33. O Lord, cause every believer to be a doer of the Word and not simply a hearer of the Word.

34. Lord, reveal anything that is not pleasing to you in our Church in Jesus' name

35. O Lord, remove anything that is hindering the Church from experiencing a genuine working of the Holy Spirit in revival in Jesus' name.

36. O Lord, fill church members with a burning desire to fast, pray and share the good news with the lost.

37. O Lord, give believers a deeper love for the Lord Jesus Christ.

38. Merciful God release the angels of goodness and mercy to defend the Church by day and by night.

39. O Lord, prosper and establish every church member in righteousness in Jesus' name.

DAY 5

A CRY FOR HELP

"They cried to You, and were delivered; They trusted in You, and were not ashamed" (Ps.22:5).

God has gathered us on this Mountain of Restoration to do a great work in our lives, our families and our nation. One thing that will cause Him to come down for our healing and restoration is our desperate cry for help.

7 Reasons Why I Believe Help Will Come from Above

1. God is a covenant Keeping God:
"He remembers His covenant forever, The word which He commanded, for a thousand generations" (Ps.105:8).

The Old Testament is the old covenant that God made through the blood of animals with the children of Israel, to become their God and they His people. The New Testament is a new covenant that God has established with all mankind through the blood of Jesus Christ, to become the God and Father of all those who believe.

In the OT God established a number of covenants with Abraham and each time a new covenant was enacted, Abraham experienced spiritual and physical upliftment. In the NT we have the covenant of salvation which guarantees salvation for whoeverr believes in Jesus Christ. There is no day a person will believe and accept Jesus Christ as Lord and Savior and God will refuse to save that person. Also in the Bible there is a covenant of prosperity through which God compels Himself to prosper all those who obey His word (Deut.28:1-14). There is a covenant of healing ratified by the blood of Jesus Christ (Isa.53:3-5). There is also a covenant of protection through which God guarantees protection for all those who live righteously (Ps.34:7; Isa.54:17; Mat.28:20).

All these covenants and more will work for you when you activate them. You can activate them by obeying God's word, by prayer, fasting, giving, etc. We have gathered on this mountain based on the promises of God. He will certainly send us help from above.

2. Our God sees and feels for us:

"For the eyes of the LORD are on the righteous, And His ears are open to their prayers; But the face of the LORD is against those who do evil" (1Pet.3:12).

The God of Abraham whom we serve is one who sees the afflictions of His people. He is not like the idols that have mouths that cannot speak and eyes that cannot see (Ps.135:16). You should never think that His silence means blindness. He told Moses,

"I have surely seen the oppression of My people who are in Egypt, and have heard their cry because of their taskmasters, for I know their sorrows" (Ex.3:7).

Before this time, the children of Israel were like orphans in Egypt. They kept crying until the time of divine intervention came. When that time came, God said, *"I have seen...I have heard...for I know their sorrows and I have come down to deliver them" (Ex.3:7-8).*

This is your time for divine intervention.

"To everything there is a season, A time for every purpose under heaven. A time to weep, And a time to laugh; A time to mourn, And a time to dance" (Eccl.3:1,4).

Before your page is opened, your complaints and groaning fall on deaf ears and the wicked continue to mercilessly oppress the weak. But on the day of remembrance things change. God has opened your page and help is coming your way from above. In this season God will bring in your Moses who will liberate you from that captivity. So if you believe that God can see all that is happening to you, do not surrender to that situation. Continue to please God as you pray. You will surely testify from this year.

3. Our God hears:

The God we serve is not a deaf God. This season help will come from above because He will hear your cry. The Bible says,

"The righteous cry out, and the LORD hears, And delivers them out of all their troubles" (Ps.34:17).

Our God pays a lot of attention to the cries of His righteous ones.

"For the LORD hears the poor, And does not despise His prisoners" (Ps.69:33).

You must know that His silence does not signal deafness. Before Moses came as a prophet for the deliverance of Israel, they thought God was not listening to their cries. They had been crying for quite a long time but without any divine response. When the season of deliverance and restoration finally came, every prophetic word Moses spoke had a rapid fulfillment. This is your own season. On this mountain, God will answer you and give you a testimony, in Jesus' name.

Sometimes God's silence is a test of faith. When the Canaanite woman came to Jesus Christ to ask for the healing of her demonized daughter, Jesus ignored her cries from the start. (Mat.15:22-28). Jesus went on to tell her that healing was meant for the children of the kingdom and not for dogs. She answered confidently:

"Yes, Lord, yet even the little dogs eat the crumbs which fall from their masters' table". (Mat.15:27).

Jesus commended her faith and said, **"O woman, great is your faith! Let it be to you as you desire" (vs.28).**Her daughter was healed in that same instant. The lesson we can learn from this story is that God's silence can quench or kindle your faith, depending on your attitude. This woman had a very positive attitude. She could easily have become angry with Jesus and returned home to continue in anguish with her daughter but she kept crying until she got her breakthrough.

Many people give up too quickly. They back off before the answer comes. Angels often carry miracles back to heaven because by the time they arrived, those who sent the requests had become discouraged and had gone elsewhere for answers. What is that problem that is weighing you down? My God, who is the God of Abraham will answer your cry and bring your deliverance in Jesus' name. The cry that moves God is not a cry of fear and discouragement; it is the cry of faith and determination.

4. Our God comes down:

You can expect divine intervention because the God we are praying to comes down to the rescue of those who cry to Him. The Bible bears record of many instances when Jehovah Elshaddai – The Almighty God came down and rescued His loved ones. He will do the same for you. David testified about such an encounter during which God came down and rescued him from a terrible pit.

"I waited patiently for the LORD; And He inclined to me, And heard my cry. He also brought me up out of a horrible pit, Out of the miry clay, And set my feet upon a rock, And established my steps" (Ps.40:1-2).

He came down into the fire to rescue the three Hebrew boys (Dan.3). He came down to shut the mouths of the lions when Daniel was thrown into the lions' den (Dan.6). God sent an angel to liberate Peter from the prison (Acts 12). Has the enemy bound you or your family in prison? The day of freedom has finally come for you.

As you cry to the Lord from your pit this month, He will come down for you. You may have fallen very deep into sin, or gone completely broke in business. It may look like everything is working against you. I have good news for you. Jesus Christ is the resurrection and the life (Jn.11:25). He will give life to anything that is dead in your life. This scripture will be fulfilled in your life this year,

"When the LORD brought back the captivity of Zion, We were like those who dream" (Ps.126:1).

5. Our God remembers:

Help will come your way from above because our God always remembers His people.

He remembered Rachel (who had been barren all her life) and her womb opened up. ***"Then God remembered Rachel, and God listened to her and opened her womb" (Gen.30:22).***

One thing you should never overlook about God is that He can never forgets His children.

"Can a woman forget her nursing child, And not have compassion on the son of her womb? Surely they may forget, Yet I will not forget you" (Isa.49:15).

Rachel waited for the fruit of the womb for about 15 years before she had Joseph. During this time of waiting, she went to her husband and said, ***"Give me children or else I die" (Gen.30:1).*** This was the cry of a woman who was desperate for a breakthrough. Finally, God remembered her. May your tears move God's hand in this season, in Jesus' name

The statement, "God remembered Rachel" should not be misunderstood to mean that God had forgotten her before. God cannot forget anyone. The truth about Him is that He is not moved by circumstances and human pressure. He works on His own program and He does miracles for specific purposes.

When God remembers you, good things begin to happen in your life. For Rachel, her womb was opened. For Noah, the wind began to blow for him (Gen.8:7). For Hannah, she became pregnant (1Sam.1:19). For Peter, his chains were broken and the prison doors opened (Acts 12). For Lazarus, he came back to life after four days in the grave (Jn.11). Don't give up! Your miracle is on the way.

6. Our God defends the weak:
"When they were few in number, Indeed very few, and

strangers in it.

When they went from one nation to another, From one kingdom to another people, He permitted no one to do them wrong; Yes, He rebuked kings for their sakes, Saying, "Do not touch My anointed ones, And do My prophets no harm.." (Psalm 105:12-15).

One truth about our God is that He is very interested in the weak; those whose rights are being trampled upon. God hates oppression, tribalism, nepotism and any form of manipulation that causes the poor and the underprivileged to suffer. At the end of the day He always steps in to defend the rights of the down-trodden.

The captivity of Israel in Egypt was multifaceted. They were in political captivity – another nation had swallowed them up. Without God's intervention, Israel would never have become a nation on its own. They were in economic captivity –they labored, and Egypt ate the fruit of their labors. They were in spiritual captivity. The Egyptians were imposing their gods on them. Today we have nations that are languishing under heavy yokes that have been imposed on them by other stronger nations. As the people continue to lament, God in His mercy will intervene and deliver them.

Are you in the grip of a wicked oppressor who is abusing you because you are weak? Call on the God of Abraham today, He will take over your case.

"He gives power to the weak, And to those who have no might He increases strength" (Isa.40:29).

Abraham found himself in a tight corner when Pharaoh took his wife Sarah (Gen.12:15). In those days Pharaoh was considered a god. Abraham who was a stranger in Egypt could do nothing against him, so God stepped in and released terrible afflictions on Pharaoh's house.

"But the LORD plagued Pharaoh and his house with great plagues because of Sarai, Abram's wife" (Gen.12:15).

God rebuked kings for the sake of Abraham and did not allow anyone to destroy him and his family. These attacks were satanic strategies to thwart God's divine plan of salvation.

God will not allow anyone to mess up His plan for your life. Any satanic agenda put together to frustrate your divine destiny shall be aborted as you call on the God of Abraham in this season. Are you in confrontation with someone too strong for you? Call on the Lord today, He will fight for you. Proud Goliath was killed with a small stone (1Sam.17). Just by singing, 85.000 of Israel's enemies were slain (2Kng.20). God takes pleasure in manifesting His power through the weak who trust in Him so that all the glory would return to Him. Are you in a position of authority? Allow God to use you to defend the rights of the weak. If you use the authority He has given you to crush the weak, God will fight you.

7. Our God is the unstoppable God:

Help will certainly come for you from above because our God is the unstoppable God. Nothing can stop God from exercising His will, or from finishing whatever He has started.

"Being confident of this very thing, that He who has begun a good work in you will complete it until the day of Jesus Christ;"(Phip.1:6).

Our God is the Sovereign ruler of the whole

universe. His decision is final. When He opens the door for you, no one can close it (Rev.3:7-8). He has what it takes to break through every spiritual or human barrier that is standing against you. This God told Abraham that his children would be in slavery in Egypt for 400 years after which He would come down to release them and bring them into their inheritance in Canaan. When the time for Israel's deliverance came, Pharaoh decided to crush her with forced labor and harsh treatment. His plan was to stop their growth and eventually to stop their deliverance. God counteracted this evil plan by making the Israelites stronger than the Egyptians (Ps.105:24). How did He do it? He released a special anointing of fruitfulness and multiplication upon them so that they became great multitudes. This caused the Egyptians to fear them.

Satan believes very strongly that he can stop God's plan for your life from coming to the limelight. He tried many times to stop Jesus Christ from fulfilling His destiny but failed. He is afraid of numbers, so he will employ every weapon to keep you in the minority. He wants you to remain alone. He wants your business to linger at the "hand to mouth" level so that you will lack funds to sponsor God's work. He will do everything to keep your church small so that your impact will not be felt. It is your duty to prove to him that because your God is unstoppable, you too are unstoppable. The only enemy that can stop God's plan for your life is sin, so run away from it.

In this season, the God of Abraham has released the anointing of fruitfulness and multiplication on your life. You will outgrow your enemies. You who had surrendered in the past will make an irreversible bounce-back from today. The

God of Abraham will crush any evil hand that is determined to keep you in the wilderness of oppression and misery. Open your heart today and welcome the resurrection power over every area of your life. The Holy Spirit says, "You are unstoppable."

PRAYER POINTS

1. *Father, thank you for all the covenant blessings you have made available for me.*
2. *Lord, I thank you because you are aware of all that I am going through and you love me.*
3. *Father, thank you for the anointing of unstoppable progress that has been released on my life by this word.*
4. *Lord, I thank you because you are aware of all that we are going through and you love us deeply.*
5. *Father, I praise you because the plans you have for us in Christ are wonderful and glorious.*
6. *Father, thank you for the sacrifice of Jesus Christ on the cross for me.*
7. *Lord, forgive and cleanse me for breaking any covenant you have established with me, in Jesus' name.*
8. *Lord, forgive and cleanse me from partial obedience and from any form of greed in Jesus' name.*
9. *Father, release the blood of Jesus to cleanse me from any sin that blocks my progress, in Jesus' name.*
10. *O God of Abraham, open my eyes and those of my brethren to know who we are in Christ.*
11. *Lord, hear my cry today and send me help from above, in Jesus' name.*
12. *O Lord, lay your hand on my life, business, marriage, ministry, church, and let people see your miraculous power and praise your*

holy name in Jesus' name.

13. *O God of Abraham, turn my weeping to laughter and my mourning to dancing this year.*

14. *O God of Abraham, turn my night to day and my sorrow to joy in Jesus' name.*

15. *I fire every spirit of discouragement, self-pity and bitterness out of my life, in Jesus' name.*

16. *O Lord, turn my captivity around and give me a testimony, in Jesus' name.*

17. *Lord, restore my wasted years and make me a fruitful Christian, in Jesus' name.*

18. *18. Lord, open my page of remembrance and cause my enemies to know it.*

13. *O God of Abraham, turn my night to day and my sorrow to joy, in Jesus' name.*

19. *Lord, use me to turn somebody's life around in this season, in Jesus' name.*

20. *O God of Abraham, deliver me from the pit of …. (sin, sickness, debts, fear, etc.).*

21. *22. Let the fire of the Holy Ghost arrest and banish any spirit assigned to quench my prayer life.*

22. *O Lord, bless me, multiply me, increase me and make me a blessing to my generation.*

23. *O Lord, make me unstoppable and unbreakable in Jesus' name.*

24. *25. In Jesus' name, I command any power assigned to stop me to be arrested today, in Jesus' name.*

25. *I command any dead thing in my life to come alive, in Jesus' name.*

26. *O Lord, make me stronger than my enemies, in Jesus' name.*

27. *Lord, move the church in this land from the background to the forefront, in Jesus' name.*

28. *Dear Holy Spirit, teach me how to live a covenant life in Jesus'*

name.

29. *Lord, restore my wasted years and make me a fruitful Christian in Jesus' name.*
30. *O Lord, visit your children who are in prison, who are persecuted and who are hungry for the truth with revival fire in Jesus' name.*
31. *O Lord, raise me above all my enemies in Jesus' name.*

DAYS 6 – 7

UNVEILING FAMILY BONDAGES

A problem that is not exposed may never be solved. Only what is discovered can be recovered. As long as spiritual darkness prevails destinies will remained veiled. Until the light begins to shine those who have been in darkness for a long time will never realize that their situation could be any better. One key prayer you must pray today is, "O Lord, arise and let the mystery behind my trouble be unveiled, in the name of Jesus." I believe very strongly that as we pray fervently God will answer this prayer. Satanic veils that have kept individuals and families in darkness will scatter, bondages will be broken, and destinies will open up for divine restoration. By God's grace you will access divine truth that will reposition you for unstoppable restoration.

What is Wrong With Us?
The restoration of your family will begin with the question "What is wrong with us?" You must ask that question and expect the answer to come only from God. As long as you can manage your present condition, there is nothing much God can do for you. I met a man in the city of Yaoundé who was broke and was living with his wife and seven children in a single room. If you can continue to manage such a condition, God will leave you there. But when you refuse to take it any longer, and you begin to cry out to God for that yoke to be broken, your breakthrough will come speedily.

Some people fast and pray but not yet in desperation. Your prayer must reach a critical point where

God can no longer be silent. I pray that at this time, because you will touch God, heaven will not remain silent on your case.. Jacob said this to his son Esau,

"You'll live by your sword, hand-to-mouth, and you'll serve your brother. But when you can't take it any more you'll break loose and run free" (Gen.27:40) M.

It is those who are desperate who ask God the question, "What is wrong with me?" It is only those who cannot take it any longer who can break loose and run free, in the name of Jesus.

I asked God:

In October 1994, I listened to a message on evil foundations preached at Limbe Fire Conference of that year. The message brought light into my soul. I suddenly realized that something was wrong with my family. I was in the Bible institute at the time and was unable to pay my school fees. I had only one pair of shoes and two shirts. My situation, compared to that of my classmates, was deplorable. I remember how I was the only student in my class who was sent out of school because I could not pay my school fees. That day I could not even afford a coin for the taxi ride from the campus. My immediate younger brother was at home with 4 Advance level papers in sciences all because of lack of funds to go to the university. In fact my family was barely surviving. My father, though married and father of children, was earning the salary of a bachelor and one far below his qualification. He had followed up files in Yaoundé for years but nothing good ever came out of it. From the look of things, it was clear that education beyond High School was going to be a nightmare for us.

After listening to the message, many questions began to run through my mind. So I decided to seek God for answers. I began to ask God, "What is wrong with us? Why all this stagnancy and poverty?" As I continued to pray and research, the Holy Spirit opened up to me many issues concerning the foundation of my family. I discovered curses and issues that needed to be dealt with. After collecting all the information I needed, I organized a fast on 2 January, 1995. Everybody in the house fasted. Joseph the youngest family member who was four years old fasted too. We prayed nonstop from 7 am to 7pm . We sang songs, repented, and wept before God in desperation. We prayed all kinds of prayers and God heard us that day. Something I cannot explain happened to my family that day. Ancient gates were lifted up and the King of glory came into my family. Twenty years after, the difference is like day and night. God has done wonders among us. This book you are reading is a testimony of divine restoration in my family. God will do the same in your family, in Jesus' name.

Family name changed:

Not long ago, a lady came to my office after reading *Power Must Change Hands Vol.1: Dealing with Evil Foundations*. She pleaded that I should come and carry out a family deliverance for her family. I gave them a program which they followed. While we were praying in their family house to conclude the program, the Holy Spirit led me to ask the meaning of their family name. They told me that the name meant "House of fermentation." In other words "House of desolation." I tried to find out who gave the name and why. I was told that their great grandparents were both afflicted by leprosy. Before

126

they died in that shameful state, they named their child who was the grandfather of this family "House of fermentation." That grandfather had died but his wife was present during the prayer session. This old woman told me that she had eleven children but today only three are alive.

The name of this family painted a clear picture of their situation. They were all fermenting. I found out that most of them could not marry, there were many children born out of wedlock, some of them died prematurely and they were also very poor. I made them to understand that the leprosy that killed their grandparents was already the sign of a curse on their foundation. We ministered to them and I changed the family name from "House of desolation" to "House of God" just as God did many times in the Bible.

"You shall no longer be termed Forsaken, Nor shall your land any more be termed Desolate; But you shall be called Hephzibah, and your land Beulah; For the LORD delights in you, And your land shall be married" (Isa.62:4).

Can you imagine that just two weeks after we separated, men began coming to marry the ladies? One of them told me that two very responsible men came at the same time to marry her.

This month God is changing any name that has kept you in a state of shame and disgrace. He is giving you a new name which His mouth will name (Isa.62:2). It is not just a new name that will be chosen by you, but, the fresh oil that God is pouring on your life on this mountain is coming with that name. The Holy Spirit spoke to me in 2010 during the

10th edition of the annual fast, "Gather my people and share the blessing with them." This annual fast is not just a program; it is an encounter with the anointing of restoration. *Receive the fresh oil now, in the name of Jesus. I cancel any name the devil has assigned for you and I command the name that represents your destiny in Christ to start manifesting in your life from today, in Jesus' name. Your season of shame is over. May God cloth you with His grace, glory, beauty and color, in the name of Jesus.*

What is the Bondage?

There are certain indicators in your family which I call "Symptoms of family bondage." If you can identify them and take time to pray and also ask the right questions, the Holy Spirit will lead you to some issues that you must repent about, repair, restitute and recover. The following can bring you light as you seek God to find out what is wrong with your family:

1. You work very hard but have nothing to show for the work.
2. Indebtedness is the order of the day among you.
3. Difficulty in getting married. Those who marry have bad or broken marriages.
4. Many are polygamous or involved in multiple divorces and remarriages.
5. Serious misunderstandings and quarrels. The family is in parties.
6. Mysterious attacks, diseases and deaths.
7. Different family members suddenly begin to receive revelations and end up as diviners (Soothsayers or native doctors).

8. The family is diminishing as the days go by. Some families are almost extinct.

9. No man or woman of any significance in the community or society has every come from your family.

10. Parents, children or family members are members of cults like "Famla," AMORC, Free Mason, and other village cults

11. Your father was or is a high priest of a god in your village.

12. You have been initiated into a particular secret society in the village or you participated in a group initiation ceremony like what we saw happening with young people in Bafoussam.

13. Your family has a particular family they consider as their enemy. You may even have been instructed by your parents to not interact with that family.

14. There are some sins that are common among your family people (immorality, prostitution, stealing, gambling, drunkenness, cheating, etc.).

15. Your parents have been involved in killing people.

16. The family land you possess was seized from another family. (Restitution is needed to break the curse).

17. May the Holy Spirit help you to discover these issues and deal with them on this mountain.

Let the Seal be Opened

In Revelation chapter 5:1-6, we read the story of the Lamb of God who opened the seven seals and how the four creatures and the twenty four elders began to sing a new song. As long as the seal was closed, the people wept bitterly because there was no one worthy to open it. Weeping will continue as long as darkness prevails. Things suddenly changed when the seals were opened (When the solution to the problem was revealed),

"But one of the elders said to me, "Do not weep. Behold, the Lion of the tribe of Judah, the Root of David, has prevailed to open the scroll and to loose its seven seals" (Rev.5:5).

Stop weeping; I have good news for you. The Lion of the Tribe of Judah has prevailed over the enemies of your family. The seal that has kept you in bondage till now is opened, in the name of Jesus. From today, let the secret behind your troubles be exposed. Let the truth of the gospel take over every dimension of your family. From October 2015, you and your family will begin to sing a new song.

The truth that sets free:

Jesus said, *"And you shall know the truth, and the truth shall make you free" (Jn.8:32).*

Your problem has a solution, which I call "The truth that sets free." Your captivity has a way out. That closed door before you has a key. "The truth that sets free" is God's solution to any human problem. How do you access this truth if the seal is not opened for you? Hear the word of the Lord for you. He says, "I lift up every veil that has covered you and your family till now. Your season of light has come. Arise and shine!"

Your heart cry should be that God should grant you grace to find your way out of your captivity. So after asking the question "What is wrong with us?" you must ask the next important one, "What must we do?" Knowing the root cause of a problem is not sufficient. That knowledge should lead you to wise action. I pray for you now.

Receive fresh light for your breakthrough, in Jesus' name. No matter how complex your case may be, let God's angel of deliverance and restoration step in and assist you to break through, in Jesus' name. May help for your deliverance and total restoration come to you from above, in Jesus' name. Receive fresh light and oil to begin to succeed in those areas you have been failing in, in Jesus' name.

Don't behave like the ungodly:
"The wicked flee when no one pursues, But the righteous are bold as a lion" (Prov.28:1).

One mark of ungodly people is fear. The Bible says they run even when no one is after them. Many families have been torn apart because of this ungodly behavior. People keep accusing one another of being the cause of their problems. For such people when we talk about exposing family bondages the first thing that crosses their minds is, "Who is that person sitting on our blessings?"

The Bible truth is that no human being has the power to stop your destiny (Isa.54:17; Luke 10:19). No witch can kill you without God's permission. So if a witch or a wizard is sitting on your destiny, the question is "Who gave him the permission?" It all boils down to you. You give him the permission when you either break the commandments of God or when you refuse to walk by the principles of God's word. So instead of accusing people of stopping you, please rise up and put your life in order. Begin to obey God's word to the letter and see how the enemies of your destiny will all crash before you.

When Israel was walking in obedience no witch or wizard could stop them. Listen to the testimony of Balaam, an international occultist who was brought to curse the family of Israel.

"How shall I curse whom God has not cursed? And how shall I denounce whom the Lord has not denounced?... For there is no sorcery against Jacob, Nor any divination against Israel. It now must be said of Jacob And of Israel, 'Oh, what God has done" (Num.23:8, 23).

Until God curses you, no man or woman can curse you. No juju power can stop a child of God who is walking in His will. They can only stop a child of God who is ignorant. Build your faith on the word of God and not on human traditions and superstition.

So as you pray today, focus on receiving light concerning the root cause of your problem; and that light should lead to a permanent solution. Ask God for the truth that sets free. Believe that this is your season of breakthrough and restoration. Commit yourself from now to obey God fully as he guides you.

PRAYER POINTS

1. *Father, I thank you for choosing me to become your own in Jesus Christ.*
2. *O Lord, I praise your name because Jesus Christ paid a full price for my total deliverance and restoration.*
3. *My Father, I honor you because finally my season of total restoration has come.*
4. *Holy Father, forgive me for tolerating any form of sin in my life, in Jesus' name.*
5. *My Father, let your righteous right hand lift me and my family members out of any pit of stagnation and position us on the mountain of change, in Jesus' name.*
6. *Father, because the blood of Jesus was shed for me on the cross as a*

price for my deliverance, I break out of any spiritual prison today, in Jesus' name.

7. O Lord, arise and let prisons holding my family members in spiritual darkness catch fire, in Jesus' name.

8. Let any evil power that has vowed to keep us in any evil prison scatter by fire, in Jesus' name.

9. You veil of darkness over my family, scatter by fire, in Jesus' name.

10. Let darkness turn into light in my family, in Jesus' name.

11. Lord, Jesus Christ I praise you because you have prevailed over the enemies of my family.

19. O God, arise and let any evil seal that has marked my family for destruction be broken, in Jesus' name.

20. O ye gates of my family, open up today let the king of glory come in, in Jesus' name.

21. I command any gate shut against my destiny and that of my family to open today, in Jesus' name.

22. Let deep generational secrets concerning my family be exposed, in Jesus' name.

23. O Lord, cause all what could not be known concerning us to be known, in Jesus' name.

24. My Father, My Father, arise and let the mystery behind my problem be unfolded, in Jesus' name.

25. O God, oil my senses to understand the truth I need for my breakthrough.

26. Father, reveal to us any step we must take for our breakthrough, in Jesus' name.

27. Father, baptize me with the spirit of obedience and cause me to love your will, in Jesus' name.

DAYS 8 – 10

BREAKING THE FOUNDATION OF IDOLATRY

One of the major causes of bondages in families is the foundation of idolatry. Two years ago, I had a vision in which the Lord showed me a dark cloud hanging over some people and families. He told me that the cloud was the result of centuries of idolatry. He showed me how many are languishing under poverty, diseases, divorces, and immorality because of this evil cloud. Deuteronomy 28:23-24 describes what I am talking about very graphically;

"And your heavens which are over your head shall be bronze, and the earth which is under you shall be iron. The LORD will change the rain of your land to powder and dust; from the heaven it shall come down on you until you are destroyed"

What do you think would happen if the heavens over you became bronze and your rain became powder and dust? It is clear; untold hardship and fruitless labours would become the order of the day. The Lord told me that the reason why some people cannot persevere in the Christian faith for long, some are very poor and miserable, and some who have been called into ministry cannot excel, is the negative effects of idolatry. He said that until this dark cloud is broken over individuals, families and the land, many lives will never blossom. Destinies will continue to be truncated by the powers of darkness. I pray that God will open your mind to understand what I am talking about. If people could understand the physical and spiritual consequences of bowing before idols, many would desist from idolatry. The sad thing is that the devil has blinded people with a veil of deception. Blind theologians tell the people "Don't throw away your tradition. Every people group has her tradition." Some call the worship of those dirty idols their "cultural heritage." At the time when communities are supposed to begin to unanimously banish the idols and the wicked practices associated to them, cultural revivalists are digging out and restoring those that had been cast away.

So the war against idolatry is very urgent and severe. I pray that the Holy Spirit will open your eyes to see what I am talking about. We must begin by looking at idolatry from God's point of view and not just from a cultural and an anthropological perspective. Learn to look beyond the statue and see the evil spirit that is manipulating the worshippers of the idol. Just take a careful look at your community of origin and find out the fate of chronic idol worshippers, together with their children. Find out what is going on in the families of those who champion idolatry and juju practices. You will discover that bondages are very rampant among them.

The Lord is calling us to declare war against any form of idolatry. We must arise and fight until the foundations of idol worship in our lives, families, communities and the nation are crushed. As we pray, the forces of darkness behind the idols shall be arrested. The slaves of those idols who are our family members or tribes' people will be liberated. God's mighty river of restoration will begin to flow in our lives.

What is an Idol?

The Encarta Dictionary gives three meanings of the word "idol": somebody or something greatly admired or loved, often to excess; something that is worshipped as a god, e.g. a statue or carved image; and an object of worship other than the one true God. Biblically, an idol is anything that has occupied God's place in the life of a human being.

Types of Idols

1. Personal Idols:

Some individuals or families have statues, trees, stones, rings, bags, etc. as personal idols. They go to these idols to do incantations or to offer sacrifices. Some of these idols are stationed in one place while others are carried around. Some individuals even have rooms in their houses dedicated to spirits. Often some family members are not permitted to enter such rooms. It does not matter what those practices generate for you in terms of money or power, the truth is that they are idols. They provoke God's wrath against you.

2. Personal Modern Idols:

Anything or somebody you greatly admire or love to excess is an idol in this category. These people or things occupy God's place in your life. Examples are: sports, games, sport stars, music and music stars, material possessions, sex, alcohol, tobacco, drugs, the only child you have, etc. I discovered that around our cities, some people go for sporting activities every Sunday morning but never go to Church. Sports on Sunday morning have become a religion to such people. The word of God commands us in strong terms to fight idolatry.

"Therefore <u>put to death</u> your members which are on the earth: fornication, uncleanness, passion, evil desire, and covetousness, which is idolatry" (Col.3:5).

Stamping out idolatry from our lives, families and the nation is a "do or die" matter. The word of God says, "Put to death." This means it is going to take violence and determination to get victory. On the other hand, those who condone idolatry will be destroyed.

3. Family Idols:

Most families in this nation have their family idols. Family members occasionally come together to offer sacrifices to these idols. Usually these idols are either representations of some gods or of their ancestors. Examples are: sacred trees, family shrines, stones, skulls of the dead, snakes, statues, graves, rivers, etc. Generally a family member is appointed to serve as a priest of the family idol. The families that have such idols have priests who serve them.

Some Christians who are involved in serving these idols hold the philosophy of "Give to Caesar what belongs to Caesar and to God what belongs to God." This is syncretism and it is devilish. You cannot worship both God and the devil at the same time.

"Rather, that the things which the Gentiles sacrifice they sacrifice to demons and not to God, and I do not want you to have fellowship with demons. What am I saying then? That an idol is anything, or what is offered to idols is anything? You cannot drink the cup of the Lord and the cup of demons; you cannot partake of the Lord's table and of the table of demons. Or do we

provoke the Lord to jealousy? Are we stronger than He?" (1Cor.10:19-21).

If you have chosen to serve the Lord Jesus Christ, you MUST make your new position known to your family members. They may persecute you because of your decision. Stand your ground like Apostle Peter and John who said,

"Whether it is right in the sight of God to listen to you more than to God, you judge" (Acts 4:19). "We ought to obey God rather than men" (Acts 5:29).

4. Tribal and national idols:

Every village in our nation has their idols. Seasonally the villagers gather there to offer sacrifices to them. In some cases the chief priest goes on behalf of the whole tribe. Some nations have their national idols (gods) too. In modern times, instead of banishing these idolatrous practices that have polluted our communities for generations, cultural revivalists have renamed them "our cultural identity." They argue that if these idols and their shrines are erased, then the people would lose what makes them who they are. This type of thinking is distorted by the devil. No wonder the Bible says,

"And those who make and worship them [idols] are just as foolish as their idols are" TLB.

It is true that man is a worshipper by nature and as such desperately needs a god. Why can our communities not reject these dead idols and adopt the living God; the God of the Bible, as our God? I know very well that most advocates of idolatry in our communities do so not because of its benefits to the people but because of what they gain out of it. Paul's ministry in Ephesus was so powerful that multitudes abandoned the worship of the national goddess Diana and turned to Jesus Christ. There was public destruction of statues and books associated with Diana worship. Now hear what Demetrius, one of those who spearhead this idolatrous industry said,

"Men, you know that we have our prosperity by this trade. Moreover you see and hear that not only at Ephesus, but throughout almost all Asia, this Paul has persuaded and turned away many people, saying that they are not gods which are made with hands. So not only is this trade of ours in danger of falling into disrepute, but also the temple of the great goddess Diana may be despised and her magnificence destroyed, whom all Asia and the world worship" (Acts 19:25-27).

You see that the riot that broke out instigated by Demetrius was not a fight for the interest of the community, but was fuelled by greed. Is it not the same thing that is going on in our communities? Those who eat from the altars of these dead gods will not accept that idolatry is evil. They will rather argue that it is not correct to abandon the tradition of the ancestors.

I thank God because the light of the gospel is beginning to shine everywhere in this land. A day is coming when the elders of villages and clans will gather to officially hand over their communities to the living God. They will officially divorce with their tribal idols and destroy their altars and shrines. Revival will break out in such communities. The fortunes of families and tribes that have been imprisoned by the devil will be restored.

Terrible Consequences of Idolatry

You should know that any form of idolatry is a gross violation of God's commandments. God has commanded us to not own or worship any type of idol. Throughout the Bible He has revealed to us the terrible consequences of Idolatry.

"I am the LORD your God . . . You shall have no other gods before Me. You shall not make for yourself a carved image, or any likeness of anything that is in heaven above, or that is in the earth beneath, or that is in the water under the earth; you shall not bow down to them nor serve them. For I, the LORD your God, am a jealous God, visiting the iniquity of the fathers on the children to the third and fourth generations of those who hate Me," (Ex.20:2-5).

Many years ago when I was still a kid in the village , I noticed that often whenever someone was very sick and it was believed to be a witchcraft attack, a certain horn was brought out for a deliverance ritual. A man would blow the horn and people in the compound and the neighbourhood would begin to yell very loudly. It was believed that, the yelling scared the witches away from the sick person. In some cases the condition of the sick person was reversed almost immediately. Recently, I interviewed an old notable in the village about this famous horn. He told me something pathetic about it. He told me that these horns were handed down by ancestors who lived many generations ago. He said the horns are powerful because they were prepared in a very special way. A certain number of human beings and dogs were slaughtered on the horn to make it spiritually powerful.

Two things happen when such rituals are carried out.

First, curses come on the community for shedding innocent blood. Second, strong evil covenants are established with demons. These demons take charge of the destinies of individuals, families and communities. It takes one who can see from God's perspective to understand what I am talking about. The old notable also told me another story about a certain wealthy man who in those days had very beautiful daughters. He said some influential villagers teamed up and killed the man by burying him alive. He said these men did this to ensure that they all bore the responsibility for the murder. They reasoned that if one of them struck the man to death, he would have been more involved than the others. They went on and shared out his nine daughters and his property among themselves. He went on to recount what happened to the lineage of each of the men who participated in the killing of the man. It was sad to hear the calamities that befell their offspring. Some of their families are extinct today.

In our communities such demonic objects, altars and shrines are very common. Take time and understand where you are coming from. Consciously deal with such issues if you identify them in your family.

What Idolatry does.

1. Idolatry provokes God to jealousy (Ex.20:5).
2. Idolatry brings punishment, even upon innocent children up to the fourth generation (Ex.20:5).
3. Idolatry will cause God to reject you (1Sam.15:23).
4. Those who turn to idols will suffer what they are running away from (Isa.66:4).
5. Those who turn to idols shall be consumed (Isa.66:17).
6. Idolatry makes people dull-hearted (Jer.10:8).

7. Idol worshippers shall end up in shame and disgrace (Hos.10:6).

8. Idols will cause God to abhor or detest you (Lev.26:30).

9. Those who worship idols are punished with anger (Deut.32:21).

10. Idols provoke God to anger (1Kgs.16:26).

11. Idol worship will cause you to do abominable things (1Kgs.21:26).

12. Idols will cause you to abandon God (2Kgs.17:15).

13. Idols ensnare (entangle) those who worship them (Ps.106:36).

14. Idols will fail you in time of trouble (Isa.31:7).

15. Shame, disgrace and confusion follow those who worship idols (Isa.45:16).

16. Double punishment is reserved for those who worship idols (Jer.16:18).

17. Idols will cause you to stumble on the way (Jer.18:15).

18. Idol worship causes insanity (madness) (Jer.50:38).

19. Idol worship causes premature death (Eze.6:4-5, 22:4).

20. Idols defile a person (Eze.20:31).

21. Idols will cause God to pour out His fury on the land (Eze.36:18).

22. Idol worship will cause God to raise His hand against you (Eze.44:12).

God has not changed His mind concerning idolatry – He still hates it. From the above consequences of idolatry, you can now understand why some individuals, families, tribes and nations are suffering from all sorts of calamities. What people call natural disasters sometimes are divine judgments released by God to punish idolatry.

Spiritual research results:

The table below shows the results of a scientific research carried out by Dr. D.K. Olukoya during a period of 30 years – sampling 500 ministers of the gospel. It shows the effects of family foundations (background) on ministry. May this cause you to reflect on your own life.

Family Back Ground	Failure Rate
1. Ministers who bear the names of the occult (idols)	80%
2. Converted occultists who became ministers	50%
3. Ministers from riverine background (those who worship water spirits)	80%
4. Ministers whose parents served Satan (idol priests, witchdoctors, etc.)	90%
5. Ministers who happen to be pastors children	30%
6. Ministers whose parents were possessed	85%
7. Ministers from nominal Christian Parents	60%
8. Ministers who converted from Islam	60%
9. Ministers from polygamous homes	75%
10. Ministers whose parents are born again	9%

How to Deal with Idols

1. Identify them:

This is the first step to deal with idolatry. Do a check from personal idols in your life to those around you that you must deal with. Also identify the idols of your family, tribe and your nation.

2. Repentance:

Ask God to forgive you for involving yourself in idolatry

either directly or indirectly. Plead for God's mercy upon your family and tribe. We have forgiveness in the blood of Jesus (Eph.1:7; 1Pet.1:18-19; 1Jn.1:9).

3. Destroy them:

God has commanded us to destroy all idols by fire. He orders us to put to death even the idols of our hearts.

"Therefore put to death your members which are on the earth: fornication, uncleanness, passion, evil desire, and covetousness, which is idolatry" (Col.3:5).

"But thus you shall deal with them: you shall destroy their altars, and break down their sacred pillars, and cut down their wooden images, and burn their carved images with fire" (Deut.7:5).

This is what you should do:

a. Commit yourself not to satisfy any sinful desires that crop up in your heart. For example, there are TV programs and other entertainment activities that fan to flame some sins in your life. You must deliberately stop those activities. When you do, the passions will die.

b. Any physical object which is an idol should be burnt in fire. Denounce them and the spirits behind them before burning them. If for any reason you fail to destroy any idol that is directly under your authority, Satan will take advantage of you.

c. There are some idols that you cannot handle. It may be because of fear or you may not just know what to do. Call for a deliverance minister to help you. But watch out against people who keep telling you, "As I was praying I saw a pot buried in your compound." If you are not careful, you will dig your house down looking for things that have been buried by witches and wizards as they say. If there are spiritual things revealed by the Holy Spirit, we should handle them spiritually – in prayer. We are not native doctors who dig everywhere. Watch out!

d. There is a procedure to destroy a family idol:

i.) If you are a family head who is the custodian of the family god, you have to inform your family members before you destroy it. Convince them to see the reason why the idol should be destroyed. When this is done, there is a likelihood that most of them will cooperate. Still some may refuse. You can go on and destroy the idol based on the agreement which you have with some family members, and also based on your spiritual authority as the head of the family. In Israel, in those days each king who came to power made a choice to either destroy idols or multiply them. Let the Holy Spirit help you. This year we burnt family idols in Mendankwe - Bamenda. This family came together and decided to surrender to Jesus Christ. After praying for them, they asked me to destroy the family gods. Very few of them did not' agree. While the elderly family members were still trying to convince the few who were resisting, one of the men went out and brought an axe. He said, "For many generations this family has been worshipping these idols, what good have they done to us? Instead we are in pain and misery." He began to crush the altar. That is how the others joined in and everything was dug out and burnt.

ii.) You can also arrange a meeting during which a

pastor should talk to the family concerning the negative consequences of idolatry and how to deal with them. Education is very important.

iii.) In some cases, the family people become so violent that even as a family head, you have to wait and pray until the Holy Spirit opens the door for you to destroy the idol. The issue is not just about destroying the idols, but also winning them to Jesus.

iv.) As an ordinary member of the family, you should not destroy your family god without the permission of the family head. You have to first convince the family head. This may not be a final rule because the Spirit of the Lord can still lead you in a different way.

v.) In case you cannot destroy the family god, you should openly denounce it in your prayer and then inform the entire family that you are no longer a part of the idols. Tell the priest of the god not to mention your name when they gather to worship it. God will never hold you responsible for an idol that you have no power to destroy, and that you have denounced from your heart. If God is not condemning you concerning the idol then the demons behind it have no right to attack you. Many Christians live in fear because they always think that things are not working well for them because of something somewhere. Please change your mind-set. Yesterday things were not working because you were an idol worshipper. God was against you at that time. But now this will work because you are a worshipper of Jesus and *"If God be for you, who can be against you?" (Rom.8:31).*

Your declaration from today should change from "Things are not working because" to "THINGS WILL WORK BECAUSE…" As for me I know that things must work because, I am a child of God, … Jesus is in me …. I am highly favoured…. I am blessed, etc.

4. Dedicate yourself to God:
Dedicate yourself entirely to God after you must have destroyed the idol. Decide to worship only Him the rest of your life.

"You shall have no other gods before Me" (Ex.20:3).
"And you shall love the LORD your God with all your heart, with all your soul, with all your mind, and with all your strength" (Mark 12:30).

If after destroying your idols, you fail to dedicate yourself or your family to please God, you have still left an opening for Satan to continue to harass you. When you dedicate yourself to please God, His blessings begin to manifest on you. He says,

"Come now, and let us reason together…If you are willing and obedient, You shall eat the good of the land; But if you refuse and rebel, You shall be devoured by the sword"; For the mouth of the LORD has spoken" (Isa.1:18-20).

Spiritual Warfare Against Idolatry
The Bible reveals that idols have dirty evil spirits masquerading behind them. Whenever you offer sacrifices to idols you enter into fellowship directly with demons, whether consciously or not.

"Rather, that the things which the Gentiles sacrifice they sacrifice to demons and not to God, and I do not want you to have fellowship with demons" (1Cor.10:20)

For you to be free from the covenants that have been established between you and the spirits behind the idols, you have to engage in aggressive spiritual warfare. The sad thing is that some people think that they are automatically free because they have refused to go back to the village for idol worship. It does not work like that. Think about this. If you owed me some money and you relocated to America without settling the debt, does you relocation cancel the debt? The answer is NO. For you to be free from the debt you must settle it.

For you to break free from the evil covenants with the idols, you must receive the new covenant in the blood of Jesus Christ and engage it to break all the other evil covenants. This is what I call the "Law of the superior covenant." By this I mean that the superior covenant swallows up the inferior covenant. Every other covenant in the world submits to the superior covenant which is established between God and the believer through the blood of Jesus Christ.

"knowing that you were not redeemed with corruptible things, like silver or gold, from your aimless conduct received by tradition from your fathers, but with the precious blood of Christ, as of a lamb without blemish and without spot" (1Pet.1:18-19).

Child of God, you have already been redeemed, and not that you are still to be redeemed. Do not pray like someone who is seeking salvation, but pray like one who possesses salvation already. That is why the Bible says *"Knowing that you were redeemed."* You have to know and go on to pray with knowledge.

Do not forget that there is no neutral ground in this matter – you are either standing as a believer on Jesus' victory or as an unbeliever exposed to demonic harassments. Sometimes the demons behind the idols will try to resist your freedom. You must resist them aggressively in faith, prayer and fasting until they surrender completely.

Do not be Afraid of Idols

Many people have succumbed to demons because of fear and superstition. A child of God should never be afraid of idols, charms, juju, witches, wizards or even demons. Why?

1. Satan who is the master of the kingdom of darkness has been defeated totally by Jesus Christ on cross (Col.2:14-15). His authority over the believer was totally destroyed (Heb.2:14-15). If you are afraid of him and his agents then you are implying that Jesus' death on the cross had not effect.

2. In Christ Jesus, God has raised you to a privileged place of authority and power. You are seated with Christ far above principalities and powers (Eph.1:18-21; 2:5-6). The powers of darkness are commanded by heaven to submit to you by virtue of your spiritual position in Christ.

3. You have been given the authority to trample upon Satan and all his powers (Luke 10:19; Mark 16:17-18). Jesus Christ declared that NO power of darkness will hurt you as you exercise your authority over them. So why are you afraid?

4. Demons respect and fear believers. In Ephesus, they confessed, *"Jesus I know, and Paul I know; but who are you?" (Acts 19:15).* If you are truly born again and obey the word of God, then no demon can touch you.

5. At the mention of the name of Jesus Christ all demons bow (Philp.2:9-11). Demons will bow out when you challenge them in the name of Jesus.

6. Idols are illegitimate before God, so heaven backs those who fight idolatry (Ex.20:2-6).
7. God the Father, God the Son and God the Holy Spirit as well as the angels are with you. The Bible says, *"If God be for you, who can be against you?" (Rom.8:31).*

You should never let fear stop you from doing the will of God. In April 1999, I ministered to a notable of one of the villages in Bafang. This man who had already written his will and was waiting to die was delivered by the power of God as we prayed for him. Two weeks after that I told him that we had to go to his village and deal with his idols. As I began to burn the idols, curious villagers shocked by what they saw said I was going to die. That was sixteen years ago, and today I am still alive. Two years ago we went to Batcham village in the West Region of Cameroon and there we dismantled and burnt down altars dedicated to the worship of skulls. Onlookers said the gods were going to kill us but nothing happened. We have burnt all sorts of idols and charms in the name of Jesus. This is in obedience to God's word in Deuteronomy 7:5,

"You shall destroy their altars, and break down their sacred pillars, and cut down their wooden images, and burn their carved images with fire."

Labour for the deliverance of your family, community, tribe and nation

It is the responsibility of all those who have experienced deliverance from idolatry and demonic oppressions, to help their family members and communities to also see the light. You have to fast and pray for them. Also look for opportunities to preach to them and share your deliverance experience with them. Offer copies of our books to them so that they can read and be enlightened.

All of us must fight the war against idolatry because its negative consequences affect everyone. The violence in our society, ritual killings and crime that have their roots in idolatry, are affecting everybody. Do not be indifferent at this time when the battle is becoming more serious than ever.

During the next few days, take time and really deal with these issues in prayer. The impact is greater when you pray as a family.

PRAYER POINTS

From your findings make sure that during your prayer; you mention the names of the idols and shrines you have identified in your background.

1st Day: Deal with the idols of your heart

1. *Lord, I thank and praise you for my life and for the blood of Jesus shed for me on the cross.*
2. *Lord, I worship you because you have set me free to the uttermost by*

the blood of Jesus.

3. Father, I praise you because the time for me to begin to walk in total freedom from the evil manipulations of idols has finally come.

4. My Father, My Father, I praise your name because whether Satan likes it or not power must change hands in my life, in Jesus' name.

5. Lord, forgive me for all works of the flesh that have become idols in my life.

6. O Lord, open the fountain of the blood of Jesus Christ and purge my soul of idols, in Jesus' name.

7. Father, let your holy finger, uproot idolatry from my soul, in Jesus' name.

8. Father, I consciously rebel against any evil that has been ruling my life (pride, lust, greed, anger, etc.).

9. Let the throne of iniquity in my heart collapse today, in the name of Jesus.

10. I command any evil thought, imagination or feeling that resists the standard in my life to break, in Jesus' name.

11. Because Jesus Christ has paid the price for my total freedom, I release my soul from the captivity of any evil habit, in the name of Jesus.

12. O Father, cause me to decrease and cause Jesus Christ to increase greatly in my life.

13. Let that thing in me that seeks to cause me to call good evil and evil good, die, in Jesus' name.

14. Let that feeling that places me in a position to despise others die, in Jesus' name.

15. Let any thought that causes me to question, doubt and argue with the will of God, die, in Jesus' name.

16. I command any idea, belief, feeling or ambition that resists the word of God in me to leave me now, in Jesus' name.

17. Any feeling that causes me to be ashamed of Jesus' Christ, be

uprooted, in Jesus' name.

18. *I reject any thought that reduces me from being God's legitimate child as well as any thought that exalts me above being God's servant.*

19. *I refuse to be anything that Christ was not and I commit myself to become all that God says I am in Christ.*

20. *Lord Jesus Christ, be Lord, Master and King over all domains of my life (Body soul and spirit) from now henceforth.*

2nd Day: Dealing with idols at personal and family level

1. *O Lord, I repent deeply from all the wicked things our forefathers have done (covenants with demons, innocent bloodshed, unfaithfulness, polygamy, rejection of the gospel, etc.).*

2. *Forgive us and cleanse my families with the precious blood of Jesus Christ.*

3. *O God of mercy, turn away your anger from my family, in the name of Jesus.*

4. *Father, in your mercy, open a new page for my family that we may live and not die.*

5. *O God of Abraham, my ancestors chose idols as their gods but I have chosen and accepted you as my God, rescue me from destruction.*

6. *In the name of Jesus, today I stand on the finished work of the cross and on the fact that I have surrendered my life to Jesus Christ and I denounce and reject all the gods and idols of my father's house, my mother's house, my tribe and of this nation.*

7. *I declare today that I will never worship you nor serve you again, in Jesus' name.*

8. *I declare that from today, I and my children, born and unborn shall*

never worship you again because the God of the Bible has become our God.

9. *I now separate myself physically and spiritually from any connection I have with any family shrine and altar, in Jesus' name.*

10. *I cancel all evil contracts established between my ancestors and demons on our behalf, in Jesus' name.*

11. *With the blood of Jesus Christ I wipe out all satanic demands, covenants and agreements with my ancestors, in Jesus' name.*

12. *In the mighty name of Jesus I cancel all spiritual marriages and dedications established with demons in Jesus' name.*

13. *I command any satanic record or register kept by the enemy against me and my family to catch fire, in Jesus' name.*

14. *In the mighty name of Jesus, I bind every evil strongman ruling my family.*

15. *You strongman, I pull you down, in the name of Jesus Christ.*

16. *You strongman assigned over my family, lose your hold over every member of this family, in Jesus' name. This is our season of freedom.*

17. *Let any ancestral or evil power from my father's house working against my destiny be destroyed permanently, in Jesus' name.*

18. *Let any evil power from my mother's house fighting my destiny, scatter In Jesus name!*

19. *Let all the shrines of my father's house and of my mother's house receive the fire of judgment and burn to ashes, In Jesus name.*

20. *I break the influences of all family gods from my life and those of my children, in Jesus' name.*

21. *I break the influences of all family and tribal god's from my life and my family, in the name of Jesus.*

22. *Let every spirit from my father's or mother's house, assigned to monitor my life be bound and cast away from my life, in Jesus'*

name.

23. *I bind and cast away any ancestral spirit that is working against my destiny and that of my family, in Jesus' name.*

24. *I pull down the altars of ancestral worship in my family, in Jesus' name.*

25. *I raise an altar of righteousness in my family, in Jesus' name.*

26. *Every limit set by the enemy on my way and on that of my family, I violate today, in Jesus' name.*

27. *I declare that my family members shall serve the Lord, in the name of Jesus.*

28. *I dedicate my children and even the unborn children of my family to God, in Jesus' name.*

29. *Let any spiritual embargo on my life and family be lifted today once and forever, in Jesus, name.*

30. *I decree today that goodness and mercy shall follow my family all the days of our lives, in the name of Jesus.*

Do the prophetic prayers now before you continue.

3rd Day: Breaking the foundations of idolatry in your community and tribe

1. *Father, I thank you because Jesus Christ paid the price for the deliverance and restoration of my tribe, in Jesus' name.*

2. *O Lord, I repent deeply for the idolatry of my people, in the name of Jesus.*

3. *O Lord, have mercy and forgive us for innocent bloodshed, rebellion against your will, and all the wicked things we have done against you, in the name of Jesus.*

4. *Father, we are guilty of turning away completely from you to serve idols and dead gods. We have abandoned the living God and turned to rivers, trees, rocks, animals, the sun, the moon, etc. as our God.*

Lord, we are sorry, forgive us.

5. We have sold ourselves and our future generations to destruction through idolatry, Lord, have mercy on us and deliver us in this season.

6. We have established marriages with demons, principalities and powers because of wealth and power, Lord forgive us and deliver us, in Jesus' name.

7. We have sold our children to witchcraft. Lord, forgive us and restore us.

8. Father, purge our land of the blood of the innocent and of the blood of animals that has polluted our land.

9. Father, let the fountain of the blood of Jesus Christ be opened over our people for purification and restoration, in Jesus' name.

10. I stand on the covenant of the blood of Jesus Christ and begin to cancel all evil covenants established between my tribe and nation with the powers of darkness, in the sea, land and the air.

11. I cancel those evil covenants and destroy their powers over our people, in Jesus' name.

12. I cancel any claim the kingdom of darkness has over my people, in Jesus' name.

13. Let every evil effect of these covenants over my tribe's people   be consumed by fire to ashes, in Jesus' name.

14. Let the captivity over my people and over this land, associated with these evil covenants be broken, in Jesus' name.

15. O Lord, let the fire of judgment fall on all the shrines dedicated to Satan in our land, in Jesus' name.

16. We bind and pull down any tribal strongman and territorial demons that control my people, in Jesus' name.

17. We bind the prince of . . . (mention the name of your tribe).

18. Let the kingdom of darkness that is ruling my tribe and community scatter, in Jesus name.

19. *O Lord, arise and let the forces of darkness sitting over the destiny of my tribe scatter, in Jesus' name.*

20. *Let the fire of the Holy Ghost roast all tribal prisons that have kept our people in bondage, in Jesus' name.*

21. *Arise O Lord, and let the doors of salvation open for the deliverance and restoration of my people.*

22. *O Lord, cause the people of my tribe to reject and destroy idols at personal and community levels, in Jesus' name.*

23. *Father, cause our tribal leaders to realise the negative consequences of idolatry and let them destroy their idols.*

24. *Father, cause our people to become tired of idolatry and let them begin to seek the living God, in Jesus' name.*

25. *O Lord, arise and terminate the work of witchdoctors in my tribe, in the name of Jesus.*

26. *Father, let the light of diviners who are manipulating my people be blotted out, in Jesus' name.*

27. *O God of Abraham, begin to manifest raw miracles in our communities and cause our people to turn away from their idols.*

28. *Father, release your anointing on my tribe's people and begin to release true men and women of God who will labour for our liberation.*

29. *Lift up your head O ye flood gates, let the king of glory come into my village.*

30. *We crown Jesus Christ as King of kings and Lord of lords in our village.*

DAYS 11 – 17

WAR AGAINST FAMILY DESTROYERS

"And it shall come to pass in that day, that his burden shall be taken away from off thy shoulder, and his yoke from off thy neck, and the yoke shall be destroyed because of the anointing" (Isa.10:27).

During the next few days we want to identify and deal with the forces that have been standing against the progress of our families. These forces have not only been opposing some people but have actually placed yokes of entanglement on them. The word of God says, "By the anointing the yokes shall be broken." So as you pray the prayer points in this section, let every evil yoke on your life and your family catch fire and burn to ashes, in the name of Jesus Christ. Break out of every evil prison and break into your divine inheritance, in the name that is above every other name – Jesus Christ.

Until the destroyer is arrested, restoration in your life and your family may remain a wish and not an experience. Why should you continue in bondage when Jesus Christ paid the full price for your total freedom on the cross of Calvary? *"Therefore if the Son makes you free, you shall be free indeed" (John 8:36).*

Not only should the power of the destroyer over your life and family be destroyed, but you should also possess your divine inheritance.

"But on Mount Zion there shall be deliverance, And there shall be holiness; The house of Jacob shall possess

their possessions" (Oba.1:17).

Liberating a captive and letting him go empty handed does not help much. That is why whenever God delivers, He also restores. He even promises a double restoration.

"Return to the stronghold, You prisoners of hope. Even today I declare That I will restore double to you" (Zec.9:12).

"Restore" is a compound word made of "Re" and "Store." "Re" means again. "Store" means to load or equip. The Lord is going to reload into your life and family what Satan has stolen from you. What has been lost for generations will be replaced again. During this program, the Lord has brought you to the mountain of deliverance and restoration. This is a season of double restoration for you. The glory of Jesus Christ will reload you with the beauty of heaven. Your soul will be established in the will of God. The works of your hands shall flourish better than before.

We are going to be dealing with the following spirits:

1. Spirit of Jealousy and Envy
2. Familiar spirits
3. Children Killers
4. Curse enforcing spirits
5. Spirits of divination
6. Anti-Christ spirit
7. Spirit of polygamy
8. Perverse spirit
9. Breakthrough amputators
10. Spiritual Marriages

1.   Spirit of Jealousy and Envy

Let us start by quickly defining "Jealousy" and "Envy."

1. Jealousy: It is that unpleasant emotion you feel when you think someone is trying to take what is yours. Those who are driven by jealousy are very suspicious. They see anyone who comes around them as a threat. A biblical example is the son of Gideon, who when he took power killed all his seventy brothers except the one who escaped. Apparently he feared that one of them could become a threat to him (Judges 9:5).

There is also a positive side of jealousy. The Bible calls God a jealous God, *"I the LORD thy God am a jealous God," (Ex.20:5).* This means that God protects and defends His people passionately. It is this feeling in us that empowers us to defend that which belongs to us.

2. Envy: It is a feeling of discontentment or resentment provoked by someone else's possessions, qualities, or blessing. It is also a desire to have something that belongs to someone else. Envy can also be described as having a bad eye on someone who is succeeding. In the heart of the envious, there is always a voice grumbling, "Why him/her and not me? Why his child and not mine?"

Envy and Jealousy Have Destroyed Many Families
This spirit is the cause of many problems that are going on in some families today. That is why you should take time and deal with what I am talking about here. This is what the spirit of envy and jealousy does in the family:

1. It attacks the destinies of family members:

Joseph was raised to become the bread-winner of the family of Jacob but hear what his brothers out of envy said,

"Come therefore, let us now kill him and cast him into some pit; and we shall say, 'Some wild beast has devoured him.' We shall see what will become of his dreams!" (Gen.37:20).

Instead of celebrating God for raising one of them to become a great leader, they decided to kill him in order to to destroy the dream (destiny).

How many destinies have been killed in families because of envy and jealousy? Many families have killed their Josephs because of this evil spirit.

2. It causes family members to slaughter one another:

This spirit is so wicked that it causes brothers and sisters to become heartless towards each other. We saw how Abimelech the son of Gideon slaughtered his own brothers. It seems some of them were even his mother's sons (Judges 9:5). This is the report of the Bible concerning Athalia,

"When Athaliah the mother of Ahaziah saw that her son was dead, she arose and destroyed all the royal heirs" (2Kgs.11:2). This wicked woman destroyed her grandchildren because she wanted to secure the throne for herself.

You must have heard all types of stories concerning killings and destruction among the children of the same family because of one reason or the other. I know a young girl who was very brilliant in school and who lost her documents because her step brother gathered them secretly and dumped them into a latrine. He was eventually exposed.

3. It breaks the family up into parties: Most families are divided because of envy and jealousy. I have met children of the same mother who are living in parties. Some cannot even greet one another. The root cause is envy and jealousy. Those who are wealthy despise those who lack, while those who lack hate their siblings who are wealthy.

Sometimes in polygamous families, this party spirit among the children is brought in by the parents. I knew a man who had many wives but who was attached only to one of them. This woman, who came in later, dominated the whole compound. The man built a good house for her and sent only her children to the best schools. He did not care much about the other children. The gap between the children of this woman and those of the other wives was too wide. The other children actually looked up to their siblings in the favored house like slaves would look up to their master. What do you think will become of the children in such a family?

Why can some families not meet in family meetings? This spirit is responsible. It has carefully established walls between the members of the family.

4. It causes lifetime battles:
The families of Jacob and Esau in the Bible became lifetime enemies because of this spirit. I have met many families like that. There are cousins – children of brothers from the same mother who cannot sit together on the same table. Some of the children grew up only to discover that their parents were enemies. They cannot really say why they should hate their cousins. Their parents just told them, "You can't collaborate with your cousins. They hate us."

When you dig this thing out, you find out that pride, jealousy and envy are at the root. In order to justify the situation, some people would accuse the other party of witchcraft.

5. It is the foundation of family curses:

Many people suffer from setbacks in life because of curses that have come on them through household wickedness. Imagine that a mother spends her time in the houses of witchdoctors to raise altars and curse the children of her co-wife. What do you think would happen to her own children at the end of the day? Curses will come on them.

Tears of pain and oppression keep pouring from the eyes of individuals in some families – orphans who have been abandoned, widows who are being oppressed, wives who have been abandoned by their husbands and children who have been abandoned by parents. Do you think God can l be silent forever? He will certainly come down to wipe away their tears.

How to Deal With the Spirit of Envy and Jealousy

1. Identify it:

Instead of trying to justify yourself, admit that your heart is contaminated by this spirit. It is not time to condemn other family members, it is time to humble yourself and plead for mercy from God (1Jn.1:5-9; 1Pet.5:6-7). If one family member will break down before God in repentance, and begin to pray, something new will happen in the family.

2. Repent about it:

Ask God to forgive you for contributing in any way to break your family through envy and jealousy. Also ask God to forgive and cleanse every member of the family from the sin.

Also forgive those who have wounded your heart in the family. My father told me how his step brother out of envy and jealousy caused him to be dismissed from school. He told me he had forgiven him because his wicked act did not stop God's plan for his life. Joseph forgave his brothers who sold him into slavery. Some people have vowed never to show kindness to their brothers and sisters because of certain things that happened in the past. Please, NO! They meant evil for you but God turned their wickedness to good. Show kindness to them so that your children will be blessed. If you repay evil will evil, curses and pains will never leave your father's house. Kill that evil seed with good. Wickedness can never kill evil in a family, only good can kill evil.

Learn from Joseph,

"And Joseph said to his brothers, "Please come near to me.' So they came near. Then he said: 'I am Joseph your brother, whom you sold into Egypt. But now, do not therefore be grieved or angry with yourselves because you sold me here; for God sent me before you to preserve life" (Gen.45:4-5).

He took good care of his brothers till his death. May God prosper you greatly and also grant you a generous heart to take care of everyone in the family, both the rich and the poor.

3. Declare war against this spirit that is behind division and confusion in your family:

Bind the spirit and destroy its influence on each one of you. I found out that children born to one woman by different men often live in disagreement. They find it difficult to live in agreement. Identify that broken foundation and ask God to heal it and connect you together.

Some families are torn apart because of the wives that were brought in by the sons of the family. Some of these women bring along strange characters and evil spirits. Athalia was the daughter of Jezebel who was brought to Jerusalem as wife to Jehoshaphat's son (2Kgs.8-9). She polluted the family line of King David for generations with witchcraft and wickedness.

Let family members who know and fear God come together and judge the spirits that have vowed to tear the family apart. Pray fervently until something happens. There is always a price to pay for peace.

4. Gather them:

Any family that is scattered lacks a leader. I pray that God will raise leaders in every family in this nation, in Jesus' name. Goliath continued to harass Israel until David showed up. King Saul was there but he lacked the ability of a leader to lead Israel against their enemies (1Sam.17). May you rise up like David for the deliverance and restoration of your family.

The "Successor" may not be a leader. He/she may bear the title but lacks the ability to gather the family. That is why I say that if you cannot gather your family together then you are not a leader. If you lack the power to do so, then you should seek God for the anointing and wisdom for leadership (Ja.1:5). If you are their leader raised by God, you must gather them. As a successor, you can identify a member of the family who has the skill to gather the people and use that person to build your family. All must not be done only by you. The fact that you have been anointed as the family head does not mean that you know all and can do all. You are a coordinator. Be wise to use the skills God has invested in your brothers and sisters.

It is going to cost you a lot to gather a family that has been torn apart for long. You have to pray a lot for them. You will also have to spend money and time to convince them to come together. Few people will want to do that because it does not benefit them per se. I pray that God will open your eyes to see the blessing of dwelling together as one in a family (Ps.133). When you understand the impact of family unity, no price will be too big for you to pay to bring your brothers and sisters together.

Take action now!

Call a family member you have not called for long. Prepare a gift for one of your family members. Just ask the Holy Spirit to lead you on what action to take to bring your family together.

PRAYER POINTS

1. *Thank and appreciate God for the gift of your family.*
2. *Thank and appreciate God for your parents, brothers and sisters and all your relatives.*
3. *Father, forgive me and cleanse me of jealousy and envy, in the name of Jesus.*
4. *O Lord, I surrender any reason I have to resent and hate my brother,*

sisters, parents and relatives, in the name of Jesus.

5. *Father, forgive us as a family for permitting jealousy and envy to destroy us.*

6. *Let the precious blood of Jesus cleanse my family of hatred, envy, jealousy and wickedness, in Jesus' name.*

7. *Blood of Jesus, avail for me in every department of my life.*

8. *I bind and cast out of my life and family, every inherited spirit of jealousy and envy, in the name of Jesus.*

9. *I forgive and release all those who have offended me in any way, in the name of Jesus.*

10. *Let anger and bitterness be uprooted from my life, in the name of Jesus.*

11. *Every door opened to anger and bitterness in my life and family, be closed, in the name of Jesus.*

12. *Holy Ghost fire, purge my life and those of my brethren, in the name of Jesus.*

13. *I refuse to be a candidate of demonic manipulation in this family, in the name of Jesus.*

14. *Arise O Lord, and let the yoke of envy and jealousy that has been tearing my family apart scatter, in the name of Jesus.*

15. *By the power in the blood of Jesus Christ, I pull down the stronghold of envy and resentment in my life and in my family, in the name of Jesus.*

16. *I reject all offenses caused by whosoever, in the name of Jesus.*

17. *Any problem brought into my life by jealousy and envy, be dismantled, in the name of Jesus.*

18. *Any power of jealousy and envy devouring this family, scatter, in the name of Jesus.*

19. *Let the yoke of oppression hanging on my family because of bitterness and hatred be broken, in the name of Jesus.*

20. *O Lord, hold our hands and deliver us from the bondage of*

jealousy and envy, in the name of Jesus.

21. O Lord, release the Spirit of love and fill our hearts with love for you and for one another.

22. Let the walls of separation in my family melt, in the name of Jesus.

23. From this day, let enemies in my family become friends, in the name of Jesus.

24. Father, restore all that we have lost because of this evil, in the name of Jesus.

25. Pray for individuals in your family.

2. Familiar Spirits

What are familiar spirits?

The word familiar is from the Latin "*Familiaris,*" meaning a "household servant," and is intended to express the idea that sorcerers had spirits as their servants ready to obey their commands. Those attempting to contact the dead, even to this day, usually have some sort of spirit guide who communicates with them. These are familiar spirits.

Familiar spirits are secretive spirits that are familiar with their victims. They are spirits that have known the family for generations. They know the sins and the weaknesses of the family.

Usually those seeking to communicate with dead family members get in contact with familiar spirits to get information about the dead. In order not to become polluted spiritually God warns us not to have anything to do with familiar spirits.

"Give no regard to mediums and familiar spirits; do not

seek after them, to be defiled by them: I am the LORD your God" (Lev.19:31).

God further declares that He will oppose those who fellowship with such spirits.

"And the person who turns to mediums and familiar spirits, to prostitute himself with them, I will set My face against that person and cut him off from his people" (Lev.20:27).

Under the Old Testament Law, those with the ability to communicate with the dead, called mediums, had to be stoned to death (Lev.20:27).

What Familiar spirits do:

1. They masquerade as dead family members.

By this they inspire lies so as to mislead and destroy family members. I know a commissioner of police whose marriage was destroyed because of a familiar spirit. The spirit always came to his wife, masquerading as her dead aunt. This spirit began to manipulate the couple terribly. The spirit finally told the woman to abandon her husband and go abroad and she obeyed. She abandoned her husband with little children and went away till today.

2. They are assigned to individuals and families.

Familiar spirits are assigned to believers and unbelievers alike to monitor, control and reinforce generational sins and curses (Ex.20:4-6). For example, if an ancestor had opened a door in the family through a certain sin, these spirits follow up family members to ensure that that sin and bondages continue. If an ancestor had activated a curse, they follow up

169

to see that the curse is executed in the family line up to the fourth generation. For instance divorce, alcoholism, addictions, sexual immorality, adultery, fornication, murder, suicide, poverty etc. Even behavioral traits such as unbelief, resisting the Holy Spirit, lust, anger, mental or emotional problems that tend to run in families may represent the demonic ministry of these familiar spirits.

3. Familiar spirits re-enforce sicknesses.
They are responsible for the re-enforcement of generational diseases. They follow the family line to ensure that family members suffer of the same problems as their ancestors. For instance, recurrent cases of diabetes mellitus, cancer, premature or sudden deaths, etc.

4. Familiar spirits are information gathering and communication line demons.
These spirits give information about you or your family to other demons to keep you from divine promises, blessings, breakthrough, restoration, and freedom. They actually set up a spy network to gather information in your life.

5. Familiar spirits attack the priests of the family. The familiar spirit will first affect the "priest" of the house, the head of the household with whom the anointing of the Holy Spirit upon the family members resides. Upon the death of the father of the family, the head of the household, the familiar spirit will pass down upon the first-born son, according to the pattern of Old Testament scripture.

When someone is anointed as the family head, these spirits seek to invade the individual, in order to influence him to enforce demonic traditions in the family. If you are a family head, you must resist this power very firmly. If you do not, even as a Christian, you may compromise with idolatry and demonic practices in your family. Thank God for the blood of Jesus Christ that has redeemed us from the evil traditions we have inherited from our ancestors.

"knowing that you were not redeemed with corruptible things, like silver or gold, from your aimless conduct received by tradition from your fathers, but with the precious blood of Christ, as of a lamb without blemish and without spot" (1Pet.1:18-19).

How to deal with familiar spirits:

1. Identify them.
2. Repent from the generational sins you and your family have been involved in. Generational sins like occultism, witchcraft, false religions and idol worship, idolatry, divination, etc.
3. Bind the spirits and break the curses.
4. Claim your freedom and your healing through the blood of Jesus Christ.

PRAYER POINTS

Take time and repent of any generational or personal sin identified then begin to pray these prayers seriously.

1. *Power of God, destroy every foundation of familiar spirits in my family, in the name of Jesus.*
2. *Thou foundation of familiar spirits in my father's house/ mother's house, scatter, in Jesus' name.*
2. *Every soul-tie I have with familiar spirits, break to pieces, in Jesus' name.*

171

3. *Every seat of familiar spirits in my life and family, receive the fire of God, in the name of Jesus.*

4. *O Lord, let the habitation of familiar spirits, become desolate, in Jesus' name.*

5. *Every throne of familiar spirits, be dismantled by fire, in Jesus' name.*

6. *Every stronghold of familiar spirits, be pulled down by fire, in the name of Jesus.*

7. *Every diviner of familiar spirits, be rendered impotent, in Jesus' name.*

8. *Every network of familiar spirits in my life and family, be dismantled, in Jesus' name.*

9. *Every communication system of familiar spirits, be destroyed by fire, in the name of Jesus.*

10. *Every transportation system of familiar spirits, be disrupted, in the name of Jesus.*

11. *O Lord, let the weapons of familiar spirits turn against them, in the name of Jesus.*

12. *I withdraw my blessings from every bank or strong room of familiar spirits, in the name of Jesus.*

13. *O altar of familiar spirits speaking against me and my family, break, in the name of Jesus.*

14. *Every generational curse over me and my family, break by fire, in the name of Jesus.*

15. *Every prison of familiar spirits, burn to ashes by the fire of God, in the name of Jesus.*

16. *Every evil utterance and projection, made against me and my family, be overthrown today, in the name of Jesus.*

17. *I deliver my soul from every bewitchment of familiar spirits, in the name of Jesus.*

18. *Every familiar spirit's identification mark on my life, be wiped off, by the blood of Jesus.*

19. I break any power of familiar spirits manipulating my virtues, in the name of Jesus.

20. Every spell and enchantment, programmed against me by familiar spirits, be destroyed, in the name of Jesus.

21. Every covenant with familiar spirits, be cancelled, by the blood of Jesus.

22. Anything planted by familiar spirits in my life, come out now and be destroyed, in the name of Jesus.

23. Let my destiny be released today, in the name of Jesus.

24. I divorce from any marriage established with familiar spirits, in the name of Jesus.

25. I break out of every family collective captivity, in the name of Jesus.

26. O Lord, let the rain of your blessings and restoration locate me and my family today.

27. Le all that has been lost to the devil, be recovered in this season, in the name of Jesus.

3. Children Destroyers

"Children killers" are spirits that target children in families in order to frustrate their destinies or cut their lives short.

What these spirits do:

1. They are responsible for abortions and miscarriages.

How many children are being killed every day in our cities through abortions? Even though proponents of abortion always present reasons to defend their crime, I want you to know that abortion is murder. You may have stained your hands by shedding the blood of an innocent baby, today is the day to repent and ask God to cleanse you with the blood of Jesus Christ (1Jn.1:7-9).

These wicked spirits we are talking about are also behind miscarriages. They try to destroy the children right in their mothers' wombs. I prayed once with a woman who had lost eleven pregnancies, some of which were almost full term. The Lord answered us and blessed her with a very healthy baby boy who is still alive today.

2. They inspire rebellion that leads to destruction in the children.
The wicked one knows the word of God which says,
"Honor your father and mother," which is the first commandment with promise:that it may be well with you and you may live long on the earth" (Eph.6:1-2).
He inspires children in families to rebel against their parents so that their lives are cut short or destroyed out rightly. As you deal with rebellion in your children, do not forget that forces of darkness are trying to use Ephesians 6:1-2 against them.

3. They are responsible for violence against children.
These spirits inspire sexual abuse, anti-social attitudes in the youths, and violence against children. Remember how Herod ordered that all the children in and around Jerusalem be killed when Jesus Christ was born (Mat.2).

4. They attack children.
These spirits look for any possible avenue to invade and destroy children. Parents keep bringing their kids who have been initiated into all types of cults and witch covens to us for deliverance. These are the works of these spirits.

The enemy is not an aimless fighter. What he is trying to do is to destroy the seed before it takes root. As parents we have to be sensitive to these evil attacks and confront these children destroyers in prayer.

How to deal with them:

1. Dedicate your children to God.

By dedication, you hand over a child to God. This is the foundation of the security of our children.

2. Teach your children the word of God.

Expose them to the scriptures when they are young. I tell parents that the first TV set to buy for their kids is a good picture Bible. Also buy good Bibles for those who can read. Unfortunately parents can spend huge sums of money to buy games and toys for their kids but not Bibles.

3. Let your family altar be alive. The time your family gathers to pray together is very important. Ensure that it is respected.

4. Intercede for your children regularly. Set aside time to pray for them and with them.

5. Deal with problems before they get out of hand.

Whenever you notice the symptoms of any problem, put a finger on it and deal with it prayerfully. When you do your part, God will step in to assist you (See Ex.2:1-10).

6. Take authority over these forces of darkness.

The basis of your authority over the enemies of your children is your sonship in Christ and your office as a parent. Learn to stand in your divine place of authority and sanction the forces of darkness that want to destroy your kids. Years ago, we had an interesting experience with our son. Every month he fell sick as soon as I received my salary. I would rush him to the hospital and spend sometimes up to half of my salary on his treatment. After going through the cycle for ten months I told my wife that we had to bind the enemy. We fasted the next day and bound the spirit behind the sickness. We broke the cycle, in Jesus' name. The child was healed and we have never had such an experience again.

PRAYER POINTS

Be specific as you pray these prayers. Mention the names of the children concerned.

1. *Worship and celebrate the Lord for the gift of children in your family and in other families.*

2. *Thank God for each one of them and for what God is doing in their lives (mention names). God is doing something good even in the lives of the rebellious ones.*

3. *Father, forgive me for failing to pray for my children the way I ought to, in the name of Jesus.*

4. *Identify the sinful practices of your children and intercede that God will forgive them.*

5. *Let the fountain of the blood of Jesus be opened for the purification of my children, in the name of Jesus.*

6. *Today as I repent before God, I withdraw any authorization I have given to children destroyers to destroy the destinies of my children, consciously or unconsciously, in the name of Jesus.*

7. *With the blood of Jesus I cancel any ground upon which the forces of darkness are standing to attack my children, in the name of Jesus.*

8. *Any power of Herod pursuing my children, be destroyed, in the name of Jesus.*

9. *I withdraw the destinies of my children (mention names) from the*

hands of destiny destroyers, in the name of Jesus.

10. I break the hold of every witchcraft initiation upon …. (mention names), in the name of Jesus.

11. You destructive power, release … (mention names), in the name of Jesus.

12. You evil power that does not want …. (mention names) to live long, be destroyed, in the name of Jesus.

13. Holy Ghost fire, burn and release … (mention names) from every evil association, in the name of Jesus.

14. …. (mention names) Be delivered from the hands of the oppressors, in the name of Jesus.

15. I destroy any arrow of familiar spirits released against my children, in the name of Jesus.

16. I destroy any arrow of witchcraft or occultism fired against my children, in the name of Jesus.

17. I command any gate of destiny killers working against my children to collapse, in the name of Jesus.

18. Every behavior contrary to the word of God, manifesting in my children, be broken, in the name of Jesus.

19. Let the fire of the Holy Ghost purge the lives of my children, in the name of Jesus.

20. I bind and cast out of the lives of my children the following spirits, in the name of Jesus.

Retarded progress – rebellion – sexual immorality – bad company – stubbornness – anti-social behavior – drug addiction - witchcraft – infirmities – perversion – alcoholism – untimely death – pride – wickedness – violence – familiar spirits – etc.

21. My children shall serve God and move forward in every domain of life, in the name of Jesus.

22. I decree that the counsel of the wicked shall never prevail over my children, in the name of Jesus.

23. *Spirit of the Living God, overshadow my children and cause their destinies to blossom, in the name of Jesus.*

24. *I declare that my children shall become testimonies in their generation, in the name of Jesus.*

25. *I decree that they shall not die but live to declare the works of the LORD, in the name of Jesus.*

26. *O Lord, minister life to my children, in the name of Jesus.*

27. *Pray that those who are not yet saved will be saved this year.*

4. Curse Enforcing Spirits

Hidden curses in people's lives serve as weapons in the hands of the devil. He uses them to torment people even in their ignorance. Until God opens your eyes, you may never know that you are laboring under a curse. Here are two good biblical examples of how a hidden curse can destroy somebody.

1. Reuben:

He was cursed by his father because he committed sexual immorality with his step mother.

"Reuben, you are my firstborn, my might, the first sign of my strength, excelling in honor, excelling in power. Turbulent as the waters, you will no longer excel, for you went up onto your father's bed, onto my couch and defiled it" (Gen.49:3-4) NIV.

As the years went by, it was clear that the tribe of Reuben was diminishing in number. They could no longer excel just as Jacob had declared. More than four hundred years later, Moses spoke prophetically against the curse;

"Let Reuben live, and not die, Nor let his men be few"
(Deut.33:6).2

The question is, "Did the people of this tribe realize that they were dying because of a curse?"

2. Abiathar:

Abiathar son of Ahimelech was the only one who escaped the sword when Saul killed eighty-five members of his family who were priests (1Sam.22). This family was under a curse of premature death and poverty, which was declared by a man of God in the days of their ancestor Eli (1Sam.2:30-36).

"And it shall come to pass that everyone who is left in your house will come and bow down to him for a piece of silver and a morsel of bread, and say, "Please, put me in one of the priestly positions, that I may eat a piece of bread" (vs.36).

After surviving under King David for about forty years, this curse still caught up with Abiathar. He lost his ministerial office and returned to die in the village in misery.

"So Solomon removed Abiathar from being priest to the LORD, that he might fulfill the word of the LORD which He spoke concerning the house of Eli at Shiloh" (1Kgs.2:27).

You can see from these two examples that hidden curses can frustrate one's destiny.

Dealing with curses:

The issue of curses is handled both in the Old and New Testaments of the Bible. Paul makes it clear that the believer has been redeemed from curses through the death of Jesus Christ.

"Christ has redeemed us from the curse of the law, having become a curse for us (for it is written, 'Cursed is everyone who hangs on a tree, that the blessing of Abraham might come upon the Gentiles in Christ Jesus, that we might receive the promise of the Spirit through faith" (Gal.3:13-14).

When it comes to the subject of curses, we have those who believe that a child of God is automatically free from curses when he or she receives Christ and so does not have to break any curses because Christ has taken them away. Another group holds that believers have to identify curses in their lives and pray to break them so as to be completely free.

I believe that certain issues of the past that have not been dealt with can still affect a believer. For example, if you owed someone's money when you were an unbeliever, are you considered free from the debt when your sins are forgiven? No, you have to pay the person's money to be free. Curses are like debts you owe people and God. There are issues you have to restitute as a believer in order to cancel any legal ground the devil may stand on to attack you. To restitute is to pay back what you owed somebody. It also means to repair something you spoiled.

Even though Jesus Christ has paid the price for your total freedom, Satan always looks for grounds to attack and hinder your progress. In dealing with curses, we address those foot holds the devil could use against us.

Other curses working against people are called "Self-inflicted curses." This is a curse someone places on himself. It can be by making a negative declaration over your life, making promises to people and failing to fulfill them or breaking your own vows to God. The words of your mouth can put you into captivity.

"If you have been trapped by what you said, ensnared by the words of your mouth, then do this, my son, to free yourself," (Prov.6:2-3)NIV.

Do the following:

1. Identify the curse:

The Holy Spirit will help you in this.

2. Confess the sins:

Each curse has sin at its root. Ask for forgiveness and commit yourself not to continue in that sin again.

3. Renounce any covenant you have with the enemy:

Sometimes the sins you commit bind you in covenants with the forces of darkness. Deal with them.

4. Bind the spirits re-enforcing the curse:

To bind means to forbid. So forbid any wickedness to continue to happen in your life or family. Tell them their time of dominion has expired.

5. Break the curse:

You have to exercise your spiritual authority at this point.

6. Decree the blessings. After breaking and uprooting curses, always decree the promised blessings.

7. Restitute:

Pay back what you owe people. After praying with a man one day, he told me that he was going to convince his family to hand back a piece of land that his father had seized from a neighbor. I have ministered to men who dumped women they had had children with and went for other women. In such cases I had to bring the two together for a peaceful separation. In some cases the relationships were restored. A man made peace with a woman he had divorced earlier by giving her an envelope of 1 million francs. Read Exodus 22 to for a clearer understanding of restitution.

8. *Change your attitude:*

Start to think and to talk like someone who is free from the curse. Speak the blessing and live like someone who is blessed. You do not have to see or feel before you know that the curse is broken and you are blessed.

PRAYER POINTS

1. *Dear Holy Spirit shine your light over us and expose every hidden secret in my life and my family, in the name of Jesus.*
2. *Lord Jesus Christ, I thank you for the release you gained for me through your death on the cross.*
3. *Lord Jesus, I confess that I have been in bondage in the following areas, (name them) and I ask you to reveal to me the cause or causes of this bondage. Confess any sin that is revealed to you and ask the blood of Jesus to cleanse you.*
4. *Lord, forgive me and my family for any sin we have committed that has exposed me (us) to a curse (mention the sins).*
5. *Let the light of God shine on the foundation of my life and that of my family and expose any curse that I must deal with, in the name of Jesus.*
6. *I renounce all contacts with occultism and witchcraft. I promise to destroy all their property in my keeping, in the name of Jesus.*
7. *I renounce all self-inflicted curses I have pronounced on myself, and I break their influences on my thoughts and my tongue, in the name of Jesus.*
8. *I renounce and break all curses I have issued knowingly or unknowingly: gossip, bitter words, anger and judgment, in the name of Jesus.*

9. *I cancel all unholy evil covenants my ancestors may have established involving us, in the name of Jesus.*

10. *I break the yoke of stinginess with my finances and I commit myself to pay my tithes and offerings faithfully to God.*

11. *Once and for all I release myself from the power of any curse (name them), in the name of Jesus.*

12. *You demonic powers involved in re-enforcing any curses in my life and my family (mention if you know) I bind you and command you to cease your activities, in my mind, body, spirit, house, family, etc. in the name of Jesus.*

13. *I stand on the finished work of the cross and I claim my freedom from all curses, in the name of Jesus.*

14. *O Lord, fill me with the love of God and cause me to serve you faithfully, in the name of Jesus.*

15. *Let fresh oil for success and progress overflow in my life, for unstoppable progress in all domains, in the name of Jesus.*

16. *Father, let the power of resurrection turn curses on my family to blessings, in the name of Jesus.*

17. *From today, let things that have not been working begin to work for us, in the name of Jesus.*

18. *O lord, because you have taken away our curses on the cross of Calvary, let your blessings become real on my family, in the name of Jesus.*

19. *Identify areas of your family that need God's blessing and begin to pray, "Lord bless …. In Jesus' name."*

20. *Father bless my family with salvation, the fear of God, wisdom, favor, long life, good jobs, good marriages, God fearing children, etc. and cause us to be a blessing to our generation, in the name of Jesus.*

21. *Let the wind of restoration begin to blow mightily on my family and cause that whatever our ancestors have lost to the devil be restored double according to God's word, in the name of Jesus.*

22. Father, arise and visit all the families of this nation and cause that satanic bondages be broken and that multitudes may turn to Jesus Christ.

5. Spirits of Divination

Spirits of divination are responsible for fortune telling, witchcraft, necromancy, horoscope, astrology, and hypnotism. All these practices are forbidden in the Bible.

"When you come into the land which the LORD your God is giving you, you shall not learn to follow the abominations of those nations. 'There shall not be found among you anyone who makes his son or his daughter pass through the fire, or one who practices witchcraft, or a soothsayer, or one who interprets omens, or a sorcerer, For all who do these things are an abomination to the LORD, and because of these abominations the LORD your God drives them out from before you" (Deut.18:9-12).

What these spirits do:
1. They possess people and use them to mislead others.

All witchdoctors and soothsayers are possessed by the spirit of divination. The Bible also calls this spirit "Python spirit" (Acts 16:16). It was this spirit that gave the slave girl in Philippi the ability to prophecy to people. Take note that what she said was true but it was the devil using her. Today we have people called prophets who are inspired by spirits of divination and not by the Holy Spirit. When you observe them carefully, you find out that they are syncretic in the way they carry out their ministry.

I once ministered to a woman who had the spirit of divination, and told me that she did not actually want to serve the devil as a soothsayer but that she had no choice. She told me that the spirit that came to her to reveal things was her grandfather who had died before she was born. She confessed that the spirit was a good spirit because it helped her to solve people's problems. I told her that it was not her grandfather but the devil, and she argued with me strongly. When I asked her to describe the man to me, she said the man who came to her was usually dressed in a small loin cloth and walked in bare feet. When she finally accepted to renounce the spirit, I began to bind the spirit of divination. She began to shout, "Oh pastor I see the man running away because fire is burning him." She now understood that she had been under the torment of a demonic spirit. The fire of the Holy Spirit will consume every chain of the spirit of divination on your life in Jesus' name.

Some people have become permanent slaves of Satan through their frequent visits to witchdoctors. You can never enjoy peace when you keep going to those servants of the devil. They will destroy your family through strange revelations. I discovered that those who regularly consult with these agents of the devil live in fear. They suspect everybody to be their enemy. Families have been destroyed because of these witchdoctors. If your mother has the habit of visiting witchdoctors then you are in trouble. She will make life miserable for you if your faith is not strong. I pray that if your mother is still alive she would receive Jesus Christ as her personal Lord and Savior and should become your intercessor, just like my mother is mine, in Jesus' name.

2. They rule families by ensuring that each generation has a diviner.
Most often when you meet a real witchdoctor, you can always trace the origin back to their ancestors. This is so because there is a strongman ensuring that in every generation there be a satanic priest in that family. We have seen people who went to the seminary to train for pastoral ministry but who finally became witchdoctors. The problem is that they did not identify and deal with these problems relating to their foundations. Some individuals run mad because they refused to serve these spirits and did not turn to Jesus Christ for protection. It may be happening in your family and you are afraid that your children may become victims. As we deal with these issues in prayer, you will never see them again.

3. They torment their victims.
Families that had ancestors who were witchdoctors or strong juju people, labor under covenants of divination. Children born of such families face a lot of hardship in life. Demons, through the evil covenants established with their parents, drain their virtues in exchange for powers. The following are common with children of such families: madness, fruitless labor, prostitution, violence, untimely deaths, near success disappointments, broken homes, barrenness, etc. People from such backgrounds struggle a lot to break through and break forth in life. Recently, along with my father, we evaluated the family of one great witchdoctor who lived in my village and found out that his family is almost extinct. The few members who are alive are very miserable.

I met a lady who fought with a snake each time she became pregnant. Her grandmother who was a big time witchdoctor had introduced her to the spirits as her successor. This lady suffered many miscarriages and sleepless nights until she came to Jesus Christ and was totally delivered from the yoke.

God has brought you into contact with this book because He is determined to liberate you from the yoke of the spirits of divination. Jesus Christ paid the price for your freedom on the cross (Heb.2:14-15). Follow the instructions I am giving you and it shall be well.

How to be free:

1. Identify them.
You cannot be free from an evil spirit until you discover that it is an enemy. A woman came to my office for prayer a few years ago. As I talked with her I found out that she was possessed by the spirit of divination. I told her that I would cast out the spirit. She refused, because through the spirit she was making some money from those who came to consult her. She left and never returned. Many people believe that these spirits are gifts from God to the family. In fact, some families celebrate their relatives who become diviners. They call them prophets and doctors. I want to say here that all diviners, soothsayers and mediums are servants of the devil. They may dress clean or dirty. They may even pretend to be Christians and use the Bible to do their work, the truth remains that they are agents of the devil.

2. Confess the sin of idolatry and worship of demons.

3. Renounce the covenants identified.

4. Bind the spirits aggressively.

5. Break their yoke over your life.

6. Destroy any altars, objects, trees, images, statues, etc.

associated with divination.

7. Go for prayer if you have practiced divination in any way.

8. Surrender your life to Jesus Christ and join a Church that teaches and practices the pure word of God.

PRAYER POINTS

1. Take time and worship God for giving Jesus Christ as ransom for your freedom from the captivity of evil spirits.

2. Appreciate God for the victory you have over the powers of darkness through the blood of Jesus Christ.

3. Repent of any evil you have identified so far and ask the fountain of the blood of Jesus to cleanse you and your family.

4. Let the blood of Jesus Christ flow over all the domains of my life and family for total cleansing, in the name of Jesus.

5. I renounce and cancel with the blood of Jesus, any covenant of divination operating in my life in the name of Jesus.

6. I stand on the new covenant I have in the blood of Jesus Christ and I judge and break any covenant of divination speaking over my life, in the name of Jesus.

7. I declare that from today, I am free from the entanglement of any evil covenant with the spirits of divination.

8. I cut any spiritual umbilical cord that connects me to the spirits of divination operating in my family, in the name of Jesus.

9. Let the fire of judgment locate the foundation of divination in my family and burn it to ashes, in the name of Jesus.

10. I divorce from any marriage with the spirit of divination, in the name of Jesus.

11. Arise O Lord, and let the collective yoke of divination over my family scatter by fire, in the name of Jesus.

12. You power of divination speaking against my destiny, scatter, in the name of Jesus.

13. *Any instrument of wickedness monitoring my life, catch fire, in the name of Jesus.*

14. *Every yoke of divination over my life and family is broken today, in the name of Jesus.*

15. *I bind and cast down any spirit assigned to manipulate my star and my destiny, in the name of Jesus.*

16. *I bind and pull down any priest of divination working against my life and my family, in the name of Jesus.*

17. *No enchantment or divination fashioned against my life shall prosper, in the name of Jesus.*

18. *Let the blood of Jesus Christ vaccinate my life against the manipulations of the spirits of divination, in the name of Jesus.*

19. *By the blood of Jesus Christ, I declare that from today I shall be an overcomer over the forces of divination, in the name of Jesus.*

20. *Let the blood of Jesus Christ speak over my life and my family and cancel any evil decree spoken through divination, in the name of Jesus.*

21. *I stand on the finished work of the cross and declare that from today the rule of the spirit of divination over my family is broken forever, in the name of Jesus.*

22. *O Lord, restore anything that these spirits have destroyed in our lives (Peace, unity, health, finances, spiritual gifts, etc), in the name of Jesus.*

23. *O Lord, raise genuine servants of God in my family, in the name of Jesus.*

24. *Lord, turn the captivity of my family and cause us to sing a new song, in the name of Jesus.*

25. *Merciful Father, from today let the cloud of your mercy and favor come and rest over my family, in the name of Jesus.*

6. Anti-Christ spirits

The anti-Christ spirit works against Christ in the family. Most family members have not surrendered to Jesus Christ not because they do not want to; they have been chained by the spirit of anti-Christ. As we pray, I am convinced that the Holy Spirit will do a deep work in our families and multitudes will begin to turn away from sin to Jesus Christ.

How this spirit operates:

1. The spirit of anti-Christ casts a dark veil over the mind:

"But even if our gospel is veiled, it is veiled to those who are perishing, whose minds the god of this age has blinded, who do not believe, lest the light of the gospel of the glory of Christ, who is the image of God, should shine on them" (2Cor.4:3-4).

The dark veil hinders the unbeliever from seeing the glory of God revealed to mankind through the gospel. The result is that they cannot believe because they cannot understand. Until the light of God shines in your spiritual eyes, you can never understand why you have to surrender your sins and accept Jesus Christ as Lord over your life.

I feel for the believers who are married to spouses who are still far from the gospel. It is challenging to enjoy the Christian life in such a condition. What about parents who are serving God wholeheartedly while their children are serving the devil? That evil veil on our family members must burn to ashes in the name of Jesus.

2. They plant the seeds of error:

"We are of God. He who knows God hears us; he who

is not of God does not hear us. By this we know the spirit of truth and the spirit of error" (1Jn.4:6).

Anti-Christ spirits plant seeds of error in the hearts of people to cause them to reject the truth. They do so through false teachings, blasphemies, etc. Family members who have received such demonic intoxication, argue against the word of God instead of submitting to it. Through the activities of these spirits someone who was already committed to the truth can backslide. I know people who were fervent believers in the past but who have become persecutors of the truth today. The spirit of anti-Christ succeeded in planting a seed of error in them.

Some of our family members have strongly embraced false religions, and some who were already on the way of truth have deviated to false doctrines and demonic practices. This is as a result of the seeds of error that have been planted in them. We have to pray fervently that these wicked seeds be uprooted from their lives so that they can accept the gospel.

It is very challenging to be the lone believer in your family. I pray that after this time on the mountain of restoration, God will raise other believers in your family who will constantly join with your to offer pure sacrifices to Him on behalf of your family.

PRAYER POINTS

1. Take time and praise God for the salvation of your soul. Worship Him because He can save to the uttermost those who come to Him in the name of Jesus.

2. Ask God to forgive you for failing to preach and evangelize to your family people.

3. *Ask for grace to take the gospel to your family and tribe's people.*

4. *I decree that the program of the spirit of anti-Christ for my life and family shall not prosper, in the name of Jesus.*

5. *Every power of the anti-Christ over my life and my family, scatter, in the name of Jesus.*

6. *I bind and paralyze the activities of anti-Christ spirits in my family, in the name of Jesus.*

7. *I release myself and my siblings from the grip and manipulations of the spirit of the anti-Christ, in the name of Jesus.*

8. *Let the veil of the anti-Christ over our minds catch fire and burn to ashes, in the name of Jesus.*

9. *I pull down any stronghold of the spirit of the anti-Christ from our lives, in the name of Jesus.*

10. *Let the power working against the salvation of my family members be destroyed, in the name of Jesus.*

11. *Let every seed of error and every demonic argument hindering us from believing the word of God be completely uprooted from our hearts, in the name of Jesus.*

12. *Let the kingdom of the spirit of the anti-Christ in our lives be pulled down, in the name of Jesus.*

13. *Let the glory of God that convicts of sin come upon us for sincere repentance, in the name of Jesus.*

14. *Let the glory of God that changes people from sinners to saints come upon us, in the name of Jesus.*

15. *Lord Jesus Christ, take over our hearts and establish your kingdom in our midst.*

Use the following prayer points to pray for family members who need to be saved

1. *Lord, in the name of Jesus, give ….. (mention the name of the person), the spirit of wisdom and revelation in the knowledge of Jesus*

Christ.

2. *Let every stronghold of the enemy barricading the mind of . . ., from receiving the Lord be pulled down in the name of Jesus.*

3. *Let all hindrances coming between the heart of . . . . and the gospel be melted away by the fire of the Holy Spirit.*

4. *In Jesus' name, I bind the strongman attached to the life of . . . for keeping him from receiving Jesus Christ as His Lord and Savior.*

5. *Lord, build a hedge of thorns around . . . so that he/she would turn to the Lord Jesus Christ.*

6. *All the children who have been dedicated to the Lord and then became bound, be loosed in the name of Jesus.*

7. *In the name of Jesus, I break the curse placed on . . . binding him/her from receiving salvation.*

8. *Every desire of the devil on the soul of . . . will not prosper, in the name of Jesus.*

9. *I command the spirit of destruction to release . . . in the name of Jesus.*

10. *I bind every spirit of mental blindness in the life of . . . in the name of Jesus.*

11. *I break every yoke of bondage over the life of . . . in the name of Jesus.*

12. *O Lord, open the eyes of . . . . . to know you in the name of Jesus.*

13. *O Lord, let . . . . . . have a divine encounter with the gospel in the name of Jesus.*

14. *Lord, save . . . in this season in the name of Jesus.*

7. Spirit of Polygamy

God's original plan for marriage is monogamy – one man one woman.

"Yet you say, "For what reason?" Because the LORD

has been witness Between you and the <u>wife of your</u> <u>youth,</u> With whom you have dealt treacherously; Yet she is <u>your companion And your wife by covenant.</u> But did He not make them one, Having a remnant of the Spirit? And why one? He seeks godly offspring. Therefore take heed to your spirit, And let none deal treacherously with the wife of his youth" (Mal.2:13-14).

The above scripture reveals God's intention for marriage. It talks about "Wife of your youth" and "Your wife by covenant." It is not wives. God warned against the multiplication of wives in Deuteronomy 17:17. He made it clear that many wives would turn away the heart of a man from serving God.

What this spirit does:

1. It inspires people to multiply partners:

Satan's goal is to inspire people to break every rule that God has established for the good of man. He who created us knows what is best for us. He gave one wife to Adam. Polygamy has never been His perfect will for mankind. Not long ago I read a book published by a pastor whom I know, and which is teaching that polygamy is a biblical truth that had been covered by the New Testament Church for many generations. He vowed that the truth must be liberated. As at now, he is married to the second wife.

2. This spirit is responsible for marital unfaithfulness:

Some people find it almost impossible to stay with one partner. They multiply concubines in a struggle to gain satisfaction. This spirit is behind such promiscuity. A man came to me some years ago and explained that there was a voice that kept telling him that he could not stay with one wife. He told me that there was a strong feeling in his heart to marry another wife. I found out that his father also had many wives, and was a womanizer.

Your problem of marital unfaithfulness could come from the effect of a foundation of polygamy you inherited. Some cases of adultery are just so terrible that you would wonder what people are looking for outside.

3. This spirit is responsible for divorce and remarriage:

The foundation of polygamy is a broken foundation. Through the influences of the spirit of polygamy many people have found themselves in the cycle of divorce and remarriage. Every time they get into a new relationship they think that it will work. But finally it breaks like the last one. Imagine the case of a man who officially got married to a lady and after a few years of marriage he traveled abroad. This man returned after some years and went to marry another woman after having dumped his wife. He fabricated a divorce certificate which he presented to the new wife to prove that he had dissolved the first marriage, which was a monogamous agreement. How do you expect such a marriage to produce a good home? The first wife who had been abandoned is on her knees crying to God every day for help. Just imagine how the end would look like.

4. Polygamy is a breeding ground for family troubles:

The families of Isaac and Jacob in the Bible went through many conflicts because of polygamy. Today it is very rare to find a polygamous family where family members live in harmony. The reason is that polygamy tries to build a family structure that was not intended by God from the beginning.

In trying to do so, people are wounded emotionally and these wounds become sources of family conflicts.

Some people who were born and raised in polygamous homes lack a clear picture of God's model marriage. Today they have difficulties loving their spouses and raising strong and godly families. They have never experienced true marriage. One lady medical doctor told my colleague that she would never get married. When the pastor asked why, she said she wouldn't want to live what her mum had been going through. Her father was that type of crude man who beat up his wife almost on a daily basis. The question is, how did this man's father treat his mother as he grew up? The foundation of your marriage is directly connected to the marriage that raised you.

How to deal with the spirit of polygamy:

1. Identify it:
If you are from a polygamous background, admit that it is a wrong foundation. Do not try to justify it. Some people quote King David and King Solomon. Find out the result of their polygamy. Their families were destroyed. They are not good examples to follow on the New Covenant. Drop whatever reason the devil is trying to present to you to make you succumb to polygamy.

2. Confess the sin:
Confess the sin of polygamy which you have either directly or indirectly committed. In your confession, consider the sins of your parents that are affecting you. Ask God to forgive you for multiplying partners if that is your case. Also check

how you have been treating your spouse or other family members in the polygamous home.

3. Restitute:

Some people have to meet their spouse or family members to make peace with them. You may have maltreated your wife, sister, brother, or children; you have to meet with them and make peace. I know men who have abandoned their wives and children and gone with a new wife. You have to make peace with them if you want God to bless you. Somebody who is reading this book is under severe judgment now because God is answering the prayers of your spouse. Go and make peace now.

Some people have to separate from the person they are living with. Even though it is painful to separate, you have to do it and return to your family.

4. Break the curse of polygamy:

Pray seriously and destroy the yoke of polygamy on your life. Also commit yourself to keep your marriage and to not divorce or add another partner. Pray for your children fervently that they would not go the way of polygamy.

5. Go for counseling:

If you are confused and do not know what to do, meet a mature God fearing pastor for counseling and direction concerning what you must do to deal with any entanglement in your life.

God has promised to bless His children who are willing to obey Him and walk in His ways.

"If you are willing and obedient, You shall eat the good of the land" (Isa.1:19).

PRAYER POINTS

1. *Take time and praise God for the gift of marriage. Worship Him because in His word He has revealed to us His perfect will concerning marriage.*

2. *Ask God to forgive you for any sexual sins and any sin that is connected to polygamy in your family.*

3. *Ask God to forgive and cleanse you from any form of wickedness manifested towards any member of your family because of polygamy.*

4. *Declare before God that you have forgiven your parents, brothers, sisters, spouse, for any evil done to you because of polygamy.*

5. *Ask God to heal your heart of any wounds inflicted by polygamy, in the name of Jesus.*

6. *Every foundation of polygamy in my family line, break, in the name of Jesus.*

7. *I renounce and rebel against any evil marital pattern of my father's house, in the name of Jesus.*

8. *Any ancestral power working against my marriage, release me now, in the name of Jesus!*

9. *I command any foundation of polygamy in my family to break, in the name of Jesus.*

10. *You fountain of immorality flowing through my family line, dry off, in the name of Jesus.*

11. *I bind and cast out any evil spirit activating polygamy in my family, in the name of Jesus.*

12. *I destroy the power of any spirit targeting me for polygamy, in the name of Jesus.*

13. *Any seed of polygamy planted in me by any means, be rooted out by fire, in the name of Jesus.*

14. *You curse and covenant of polygamy working in my life, break now, in the name of Jesus!*

15. *I cancel any power of marital failure over my life, in the name of*

Jesus.

16. I receive grace to deal with any problem related to polygamy in my family, in the name of Jesus.

17. Let the marital destinies of my family members be released from the grip of the spirit of polygamy, in the name of Jesus.

18. I command any war going on in my family and born from polygamy, to stop from today, in the name of Jesus.

19. Let the blood of Jesus Christ flow in my family and bring healing to every wounded emotion, in the name of Jesus.

20. I command all walls of division standing between us in my family to break, in the name of Jesus.

21. O Father, baptize our hearts with love and cause us to develop genuine love for one another, in the name of Jesus.

22. Let enemies in my family become friends, in the name of Jesus.

23. Let the children of my family hate polygamy, in the name of Jesus.

24. Father, by your mercy, restore to us what we have lost, in the name of Jesus.

25. O Lord, destroy the yoke of divorce and remarriage and establish us, in the name of Jesus.

26. Let our marital destinies open up, in the name of Jesus.

27. Pray for those whose marriages are sick and for those whose marriages are broken. Ask God for healing and restoration.

8. The Spirit of Perversion

The verb "Perverse" is the Greek word "*Diastrepho*" which means to distort or to be morally corrupt. The noun "Perversion" according to the Encarta Dictionaries is "A sexual practice considered unusual or unacceptable". It is also, "The changing of something good, true, or correct into something bad or wrong". This is exactly what the spirit of perversion does in the family. It causes family members to engage in evil sexual activities that lead to curses and bondages.

Leviticus 18:1-30 and 20:1-27 outline to us the different sexual activities that can pollute a family. In each case God points out the negative consequences that will befall those who indulge in such sinful practices.

1. Adultery:
A married member of the family goes out to sleep with another person. This brings curses on the family.

2. Fornication:
When unmarried members of the family indulge in premarital sexual activities. Unwanted pregnancies come in. Children are born into the family without fathers, some of whom at the end become a nuisance to the family. Diseases are contracted which finally contaminate the family line. Some end up with barrenness. The foundations of the young people are destroyed before marriage. Some of them die prematurely because of promiscuity. How many young members of your family have been killed by AIDS?

3.Incest:
Family members indulge in sexual activities with one another. There are two dimensions of incest going on in families:
- People from the same blood line – brothers and sisters, cousins,   uncles, aunts, nieces and nephews engage in sexual activities.
- Husbands or wives engage in sexual activities with the

relatives of their spouses. Sometimes when children from the families of the husband or wife come together, the spirit of perversion brings them into sexual activities. Unfortunately some parents don't care to find out what is going on in their houses until brothers begin to impregnate their sisters. Sometimes such parents have also been intoxicated by the spirit of perversion. A young man about 17 years old confessed to me that he used to stay up with his elder sister to watch late night pornographic movies until one night his sister told him that they should try what they saw on the screen. That is how they went into incest and continued until he came to a crusade and was convicted. May God open your eyes to see the abominations that are going on in your house, in Jesus' name. When pregnancies occur, parents take the children to doctors for abortions. You that doctor trying to solve such a problem by shedding blood, watch out! You are partaking in somebody's sin. You parents trying to solve such problems by killing an innocent baby, watch out! You are adding sin to sin. Blood shall not leave your house. I know it is a challenging situation but you must do it God's way.

One phenomenon that is creeping up today is that of cousins getting married to each other. In most cases the two young people defy their parents' counsel and go on to marry. This lays a foundation for curses in the family they are trying to develop (Read the Bible passage I cited above). Barrenness and other painful experiences in the family can be traced to some of these perverse sexual activities going on in the family.

4. Homosexuality:
Family members are involved in homosexuality. It is an

abomination. When you do this, you invite the spirit of perversion to contaminate your family.

5. Bestiality:
This is engaging in sexual activities with animals. It brings curses on the family.

6. Prostitution:
When family members engage in prostitution, they pollute the family. I have met many young men and women born to prostitutes with broken foundations. Many of them are struggling to survive.

Discourage your children and family members from any involvement in any form of prostitution.

"Do not prostitute your daughter, to cause her to be a harlot, lest the land fall into harlotry, and the land become full of wickedness" (Lev.19:29).

Don't accept money generated from prostitution. Even God warned his priests not to accept offerings that were generated through prostitution.

"You shall not bring the wages of a harlot or the price of a dog to the house of the LORD your God for any vowed offering, for both of these are an abomination to the LORD your" (Deut.23:18).

You should love your relatives who are prostituting but never encourage them in their abomination. When I was a kid I had an aunt who was a "Free woman." She tried in vain to convince my parents to allow me to come and stay with her during holidays but my parents who were godly vehemently refused. They told her that they would not want their son to be contaminated by the spirit of prostitution. When she finally got married and became responsible my parents permitted me to go.

7. Sponsoring perversion:
There are people who make their money through the sex industry. They sell pornographic materials to make their money. A man whose life was completely shattered came to us a few years ago for prayers. He had been trafficking pornographic materials for long and was making money but his life was polluted. He confessed that a certain strange spirit would come on him and he would engage in sex with anyone he could find or even with animals. He had had sex with chickens, pigs, etc. Just think about his wife and children.

Some spouses force their partners to watch pornography. Even if a medical doctor advised you to use pornographic materials to solve any challenge you are facing in your relationship with your spouse, please refuse. Do not bring abominations into your house. It will pollute the foundation of your house. The spirits that inspired those who acted the movie will possess those who watch them. As you read this book, the anointing of the Holy Spirit that inspired me to write is being transferred on you and will certainly affect your family. That is how these things work, so be careful!

Other people operate brothels or what people commonly call "Chambre de passe." People pay them and use these places to commit sin. There is one of such brothels in the heart of Nkwen, Bamenda - Cameroon. A young prostitute testified that she is obliged to sleep with any type of man to raise money because she has to pay the landlord three thousands francs (3.000FCFA) daily as rent for a single room. There are many of them living in the place. How much do you think this man is making monthly through this perverse business? It should be huge sums of money. The sad thing is that his family will pay for the wickedness. The spirits of perversion will follow him to his house and take over his children and those to be born in the future.

How to be free from the spirit of perversion:

1. *Repent.* Admit that you have sinned and ask God to forgive you.
2. Destroy all pornographic materials in your keeping. Surrender all other satanic objects in your keeping (Rings, tree barks, special perfumes, bangles, etc.)
3. Carefully renounce covenants with all sexual spirits.
4. Break all soul ties. Separate from the person you have been sinning with. Expose it to a godly person who can help you out.
5. Break every foundation of sexual perversion prayerfully.
6. Open up for counseling. A godly pastor will guide you out of your mess.
7. Consecrate your life to Jesus Christ (see Rom.6:13-14)
8. Fill yourself daily with the word of God.

PRAYER POINTS

1. *Lord, thank you for my life and for your power made available for me*
2. *Take time and worship Him for who He is, for what He has done in your life, family and nation. Also worship Him for what He is about to do in your life.*
3. *O Lord, forgive me for all my sexual sin with .... (Mention their names one after the other. For those you do not remember still*

ask God to forgive you).

4. *O Lord, forgive me for polluting my life with any form of perversion (Pornography, bestiality, lesbianism, homosexuality, incest, etc.), in the name of Jesus.*

5. *O Lord, open the fountain of the blood of Jesus Christ to cleanse the foundation of my family of any form of sexual perversion, in the name of Jesus.*

Lay your right hand on your lower abdomen as you pray the prayers below for yourself.

6. *Lord, today I renounce any sexual covenant established between me and .... (Mention the names one after the other), in the name of Jesus.*

7. *I separate myself today from .... (Mention the name) body, soul and spirit, in Jesus' name.*

8. *I command any evil spirit of immorality harassing my life because of my union with .... (Call the names of all your sexual partners) to leave me today and to never come back, in the name of Jesus.*

9. *Lord, cleanse me with the blood of Jesus from any defilement in my body, soul and spirit, through visits to witchdoctors, in the name of Jesus.*

10. *Lord, cleanse me with the blood of Jesus from any defilement in my body, soul and spirit, through sex with any person in the physical or in the spiritual realm, in the name of Jesus.*

11. *Lord, forgive and cleanse me from any sexual contamination inherited from my parents, in the name of Jesus.*

12. *Today I renounce and separate myself from any family covenant with any sexual spirits, in Jesus' name*

13. *I command any marriage certificate with any spirit husband/wife to catch fire now in Jesus' name!*

14. *I command anything connecting me to any evil spirit to burn by fire, in the name of Jesus.*

15. *I divorce now from any marriage I am in knowingly or unknowingly with marine spirits, in the name of Jesus.*

16. *I release myself from any generational curse bringing perversion into my life, in the name of Jesus.*

17. *I release myself from any form of addiction, in the name of Jesus.*

18. *I bind and cast away from my life any spirit of perversion, in the name of Jesus.*

19. *I dedicate myself body, soul and spirit to serve Jesus Christ in purity, in the name of Jesus.*

20. *Fire of God, make me too hot for the spirits of perversion, in the name of Jesus.*

21. *Now that I know the truth, may I never become a victim at the altar of perversion, in the name of Jesus.*

Continue to pray for your family as follows:

22. *I command any evil foundation of sexual perversion in my family to catch fire, in the name of Jesus.*

23. *Let the yoke of sexual perversion (incest, bestiality, adultery, fornication, homosexuality, lesbianism, prostitution, etc.) on the necks of my family members break into pieces, in the name of Jesus.*

24. *I stand on the finished work of the cross and the blood of Jesus Christ and I bind the strongman responsible for sexual perversion in my family, in the name of Jesus.*

25. *Every prison of perversion holding my family members, catch fire and burn, and let them be free (Mention names), in the name of Jesus.*

26. *Father, arise let sexual perversion in our homes be exposed and dealt with, in the name of Jesus.*

27. *I command you spirit of ....(Incest, bestiality, adultery, fornication, homosexuality, lesbianism, prostitution, etc.), leave my*

family now, in the name of Jesus.

28. *O Lord, baptize us with the spirit of holiness and the fear of God, in Jesus' name.*

29. *O Lord my God, in your mercy, restore the virtues my family has lost because of sexual perversion, in the name of Jesus.*

30. *Father, empower us with grace to keep all forms of sexual immorality under our feet, in the name of Jesus.*

31. *Lord arise today and destroy the yoke of sexual perversion that is oppressing our families, in the name of Jesus.*

DAY 18

PRAYING FOR MISSIONS AND MISSIONARIES

"Finally, brethren, pray for us, that the word of the Lord may run swiftly and be glorified, just as it is with you, and that we may be delivered from unreasonable and wicked men; for not all have faith" (2Thess.3:1-2).

"Continue earnestly in prayer, being vigilant in it with thanksgiving; meanwhile praying also for us, that God would open to us a door for the word, to speak the mystery of Christ, for which I am also in chains, that I may make it manifest, as I ought to speak" (Col.4:2-4).

The effectiveness of any mission endeavor relies much on the prayers of the saints. That is why Apostle Paul requested for prayers from the brethren again and again. Today, I want you to use the prayer topics below to pray for mission agencies, the missionaries you know, as well as those you do not know.

PRAYER POINTS

1. *Lord, thank you for all the missionaries sent out by our national Church.*
2. *Lord, thank you for all the missionary organizations that are ministering in this nation.*
3. *Lord, thank you for all the work the missionaries are doing for the advancement of the kingdom of God.*

4. *O Lord, create the thirst and hunger for God and holiness in the hearts of the missionaries, their spouses and their children.*

5. *O Lord, release fresh revival fire on all the missionaries and cause them to become agents of revival in the name of Jesus.*

6. *Lord, release your fire of revival on the spouses and children of our missionaries and cause them to become channels of revival in the name of Jesus.*

7. *O Lord, let there be a fresh outpouring of the Holy Spirit on the lives of the missionaries for supernatural expansion of their ministries in the name of Jesus.*

8. *O Lord, release faithful, committed, dedicated and obedient laborers into the mission fields in Cameroon.*

9. *Lord, release laborers to the unreached people groups of this nation in the name of Jesus.*

10. *Lord, open the doors of this nation to foreign missionaries who want to serve you in this nation in the name of Jesus.*

11. *O Lord, touch the government of this nation to favor missionaries in the name of Jesus.*

12. *O Lord, give to the missionaries the power for an effective prayer life.*

13. *O Lord, release upon the missionaries a fresh anointing to break down the strongholds of territorial spirits in the name of Jesus.*

14. *O Lord, touch the converts the missionaries are ministering to with a hunger and thirst for the word of God.*

15. *Let the power of sin and wickedness oppressing the people the missionaries are ministering to, be broken in the name of Jesus.*

16. *O Lord, release the anointing that brings salvation upon the people the missionaries are ministering to in the name of Jesus.*

17. *O Lord, visit all the missionary organizations in this nation with fresh zeal for your work in the name of Jesus.*

18. *Lord, visit and bless all missionary organizations that have sent*

missionaries to this nation in the name of Jesus.

19. O Lord, raise committed givers to support the missionaries in the name of Jesus.

20. O Lord, in this season visit and turn around any difficulty the missionaries are facing in the name of Jesus.

21. Lord, bless the work of Bible translation that is being done by CABTAL and SIL. Let more tribes open up for translation.

22. Lord, bless and prosper the work of missions in the prisons of this nation. Let many prisoners be genuinely saved.

23. Lord, bless the work of missionaries among street children and cause that they will be saved and reinstated into families.

24. Lord, bless the work of missionaries among the orphans and cause them to raise God fearing children. Let the activities of those who traffic children be frustrated and punished in the name of Jesus.

25. Lord, bless the work of missionaries among prostitutes and criminals. Protect the missionaries and cause that prostitutes and criminals will be genuinely saved.

26. Lord, bless the work of missionaries among the Muslims. O Lord, cause them to see the glory of the risen Jesus Christ and also protect the missionaries and their converts.

27. Lord, bless the work of missionaries on the internet. Supply their needs and connect them daily to people who need the gospel.

28. Lord, bless the work of missionaries on the Radio and TV. Supply their needs and cause that through their work there would be a great harvest for the kingdom.

29. Lord, bless the work of missionaries among students from primary school to university and professional schools. Lord, let there be a great revival and a mighty harvest of souls.

30. Lord, cause that all the Churches in this land will catch a fresh

vision for missions. Let spiritual leaders realize that the mission of God (winning) souls is the raison d'être of the Church on earth.

DAY 19

BREAKING THE POWERS OF HOUSEHOLD WITCHCRAFT

Witchcraft spirits are responsible for control, manipulation and destruction of people's destinies. A witch is someone who uses satanic powers to control, manipulate and destroy others. Many are suffering today because of the activities of witches and wizards. It becomes even worse when the witch or wizard is operating right from your house or family.

When it comes to the topic of witchcraft, there are two extreme schools of thought: We have those who believe that witchcraft does not exist at all. According to such people problems, sicknesses, and calamities can only come because of scientific reasons. As such, when they have any problem, they turn only to science to help them out. On the other hand there are those who see witchcraft behind all their problems. This is also wrong. Not all problems are caused by witches and wizards. Not all those who have been accused of being witches and wizards know anything about witchcraft. Some innocent people have been accused, ostracized or even killed in some communities because of the fear of witchcraft.

God warns against witchcraft:

God commanded the children of Israel to neither practice nor tolerate witchcraft in their midst.

"There shall not be found among you anyone who makes his son or his daughter pass through the fire, or

one who practices witchcraft, or a soothsayer, or one who interprets omens, or a sorcerer" (Deut.18:10).

The nations of Israel were greatly influenced to abandon God because of the witchcraft of Jezebel (2Kgs.17:17). This witchcraft initiated terrible abominations among the people of Israel. People roasted their children in fire, offered human sacrifices, and did other such abominable things. This brought God's wrath on the nation.

Family witchcraft:

Household witchcraft activities take place at two levels:

1. Family witch covens:

A family witch coven is a union (group) of witches and wizards who are members of the same family tree. In their meetings they perpetrate wickedness against family members and other people. The destinies of certain individuals are bound in such witch covens. Usually such witches appoint their successors from the family before they die. Many people have been destroyed by witchcraft covens. Many years ago my parents rescued the daughter of woman who was under serious witchcraft attacks in a village where my dad was working as a teacher. Out of more than ten children that this woman had given birth to, only two girls were still alive. She had been losing her children under mysterious circumstances. One of the two girls was suddenly attacked by epilepsy. So when my father was transferred out of that village, he decided to take along that little girl who at the time was about seven years old. Her epileptic sister died later. She grew up in our house and today she is the lone child to her mother. God gave her a husband and she is a mother of seven beautiful children. Her father tried many times to take her away from my family but my parents refused. At the time of his death, it was discovered that this man was the one who had destroyed his own children.

A number of parents have brought their children to us for deliverance and during the prayer sessions some of the children have confessed that they have been initiated into family witchcraft covens. Some of them mentioned the names of other family members who are part of the coven. Our prayer is that God's hand shall arise and destroy such covens that are working against your family so that your deliverance and restoration will come speedily.

2. Individual witches and wizards:

Sometimes in the family there are individuals who are witches and wizards, even though there may be no family witch coven. The devil uses such individuals to torment family members and other people. Occultism and sorcery fall under this category. Some of these evil people use other family members to make money. They control and manipulate the progress of others through diverse satanic means. One day a man brought his daughter to us for prayer. When we began to pray the girl confessed that she had been initiated into witchcraft by a friend in school. She also confessed that she was the brain behind some of the mysterious happenings in her home. Her father testified about mysterious disappearances of money in the house, a mysterious fire break out that almost burnt down their house, and terrible oppressions that were going on among members of the house hold.

On this mountain, because Jesus Christ paid the price

for your total freedom, you are breaking out of every witchcraft prison, in the name of Jesus.

How to break the yoke of household witchcraft

1. Repent:
If you are involved in the practice of witchcraft, occultism and sorcery, please repent. Ask God to forgive you. Plead that the blood of Jesus Christ will cleanse you.

2. Expose it:
The Bible commands us to expose all the works of darkness and not cover them (Read Eph.5:11; Acts 19:19-20). If you refuse to expose the devil and his agents, they will destroy you. Do not be afraid of their threats. All of that is to keep you in perpetual slavery. Expose them and see how that power over you will be broken.

3. Destroy any witchcraft property in your keeping:
See (Acts 19:18-21). As long as you keep their property, the evil spirits will continue to follow you like flies would follow someone carrying a piece of rotten meat.

4. Engage in serious warfare prayer:
Pray the prayer topics below in faith. If you are under any witchcraft manipulation, you will be totally free. If you have discovered that witchcraft activities are going on in your family, intercede for the salvation of those involved and also judge their activities. Insist in prayer until breakthrough comes. Some of these people were initiated into witchcraft even as babies, while some got into witchcraft while still in

the womb. Should we kill all of them? No. We should pray for their liberation, destroy the works and powers completely, and let God punish with death those he wants to kill.

5. Stay away from sin:
God promises to be with us when we stay away from sin (2Cor.6:1-18). Holiness is a spiritual disinfectant that keeps away demons. Witches and wizards have a hard time dealing with people who live in holiness.

To be able to stay away from sin, you must be addicted to God's word. For this reason, consume God's word as much as you eat physical food, and it shall be well with you (Isa.3:10).

PRAYER POINTS
1. *Repent from any witchcraft activities.*
2. *Ask God to show you mercy because of the price Jesus paid for you on the cross, and also based on the fact that you have surrendered your life to Jesus Christ.*
3. *Ask the blood of Jesus Christ to cleanse you and your family from all witchcraft pollutions.*
4. *Plead that God should forgive any member of your family who is involved in household witchcraft.*
5. *Ask God in His infinite mercy to open the door of salvation and deliverance for such people.*
6. *O Rock of ages, arise and let the foundation of witchcraft in my family scatter to pieces, in the name of Jesus.*
7. *Every seat of household witchcraft operating against my family, receive thunder and scatter, in the name of Jesus.*
8. *Every witch coven working against me and my family, catch fire and*

burn to ashes, in the name of Jesus.

9. *Let all witch covens raised against my family become desolate from today, in the name of Jesus.*

10. *Let the strongholds of witchcraft powers against us be pulled down by earthquake, in the name of Jesus.*

11. *Let every network of witchcraft in my family be consumed by God's fire of judgment, in the name of Jesus.*

12. *Every weapon of witchcraft fashioned against my family, be destroyed, in the name of Jesus.*

13. *Let all altars of witchcraft speaking against us scatter forever, in the name of Jesus.*

14. *I cancel every witchcraft utterance spoken against my family, in the name of Jesus.*

15. *I bind and pull down any strongman responsible for household witchcraft in my family, in the name of Jesus.*

16. *I deliver my soul from every witchcraft bewitchment, in the name of Jesus.*

17. *I wipe away any witchcraft identification mark on my life, in the name of Jesus.*

18. *I cancel and break every witchcraft covenant that concerns me and my family, in the name of Jesus.*

19. *I release my destiny from any witchcraft manipulations, in the name of Jesus.*

20. *I destroy all witchcraft weapons fashioned against me, (remote controls, evil arrows, satanic mirrors, evil poisons, etc), in the name of Jesus.*

21. *Let every witchcraft pot working against me and my family break to pieces, in the name of Jesus.*

22. *Every camp of witchcraft working against our prosperity be destroyed now, In the name of Jesus!*

23. *I break and loose myself from all evil curses, chains, spells,*

bewitchment, or sorcery released against me, in the name of Jesus.

24. Let the communication systems of household witchcraft working against us catch fire, in the name of Jesus.

25. Let any witchcraft curse working against us be reversed as from today by the blood of Jesus, in the name of Jesus.

26. Fire of God, fall and consume any spiritual snake, bird, or reptile that is an instrument of witchcraft released against me and my family, in the name of Jesus.

27. Let the blood of Jesus wash off every witchcraft identification mark on my life, in the name of Jesus.

28. Let the fire of God visit the forest, the water, the land and the air and burn to ashes any seat of witchcraft established against us, in the name of Jesus.

29. Let any witchcraft wall raised against my destiny collapse woefully, in the name of Jesus.

30. I send confusion into the camp of witches and wizards militating against us and I scatter them forever, in the name of Jesus.

31. I reject the works of witchcraft in my dreams, in the name of Jesus.

32. O Father, restore all that witches and wizards have destroyed in my family, in the name of Jesus.

33. My Father, put an end to the rule of witchcraft in my family, in the name of Jesus.

34. O Lord, turn every curse on my family to abundant blessings, in the name of Jesus.

35. Father, arise today and let the story of my family and those of my brethren change, in the name of Jesus.

DAY 20

BREAKING EVIL SPIRITUAL MARRIAGES

An evil spiritual marriage is a situation where a person is spiritually entangled with demonic spirits (succubus and incubus spirits). From personal experience in the deliverance ministry I have come to understand that some people are actually married spiritually – some consciously and some unconsciously. These evil spiritual marriages constitute the basis for many problems in the home. In order to enjoy your freedom in Christ, such demonic marriages must be identified and destroyed.

Wicked Activities of the Incubus and the Succubus Spirits

1. Sexual harassments in dreams:
The succubus spirit is usually called "the spirit wife" while the incubus spirit is called "the spirit husband." These spirits come to have sexual intercourse with their victims in their sleep.

2. Control and destruction:
They also try to control and rule their victims, resulting in broken marriages, serious gynecological problems, marital distress, miscarriages and impotence. These spirits destroy marriages more than any other power.

3. Stagnation and hardship:

Those with evil spiritual marriages go through untold hardship, financial failure and general failure at the edge of breakthrough. In fact studies show that some people in the church are tormented by these spirits. Unfortunately many are ignorant of their situation. Get the truth and be free in the name of Jesus.

"Therefore my people are gone into captivity, because they have no knowledge: and their honorable men are famished, and their multitude dried up with thirst." (Isa.5:13).

You must know that the supernatural world is as real as the physical. What takes place in the spiritual realm also affects us physically in our day to day lives.

How Evil Spiritual Marriages are Established
1. Sinful sexual unions:

All sexual unions that are condemned by the Bible (fornication, adultery, incest, homosexuality, orgies, sadism, bestiality, lesbianism, rape and others) are open doors to the spirits of incubus and succubus.

2. Perversion:

Perverse activities like masturbation, pornography, listening to immoral music, watching indecent movies, sensual dressing and use of indecent language can open up your life to these spirits.

3. Parental dedication by initiation, incision, idol worship:

Most idolatrous parents ignorantly dedicate their children to the idols they worship for protection, prosperity, longevity and knowledge. When the bodies of the children are incised and the blood of an animal is used to bathe them, terrible blood covenants are established with demonic spirits. These spirits become legal masters over the children as they grow up.

4. Inherited sins or evil foundations:
The transference of sexual sins through the (maternal or paternal) blood line opens the door to the spirit of incubi and succubae to swim in.

5. Occult participation and involvement:
Anyone involved in any occultism is exposed to these spirits. Any person whose parents participate in the occult has a high exposure rate to attacks of demons and their manipulation (Read Deut.18:10-12).

6. Cultural dances:
When you involve yourself in cultural entertainment and dancing of juju either in the village or in an urban area, you get involved with spiritual altars. If you dance before such idols you might become a bride or a bridegroom to them (Read Exo.32:5-6).

7. Unprofitable gifts:
Accepting polluted gifts from evil people can connect you to spirit husbands or spirit wives. There are people who have become entangled with these spirits unconsciously. Watch out!

8. Inheriting a satanic priesthood:

Many families have family idols or shrines. These idols are generally inherited from the ancestors. Some of the idols have been worshipped for many generations. In modern times some families have destroyed theirs. I have visited a number of families this year to burn down family idols and shrines.

One who serves these idols as a priest is married to them. The spirits control the priest very strictly.

Some Symptoms of Evil Spiritual Marriages

If you have been experiencing the following symptoms it is likely that you are entangled in a spiritual marriage:

1. Continuous marital distresses (constant disagreements, quarrelling and fighting);
2. Constant sexual relationships in dreams. Sometimes on and off;
3. Hatred of marriage (refusal to marry whosoever);
4. Strong uncontrollable sexual desires;
5. Divorce and remarriage;
6. Neglect or abandonment by your spouse (sometimes for no serious reason);
7. Demonic dream assistance (some strange person always giving you help in the dream);
8. Constantly swimming or seeing a river in the dream (marriage   with the marine kingdom);
9. Missing one's menstrual period in the dream regularly;
10. Pregnancy in the dream on regular basis;
11. Breast- feeding a baby in the dream from time to time;
12. Shopping with a strange man or a woman in the dream regularly;

13. Seeing a strange man or woman sleeping by your side in the dream;

14. Hatred by your spouse;

15. Serious gynecological problems;

16. Having a miscarriage or falling sick after sexual intercourse in dreams;

17. Constantly wedding in dreams;

18. You always feel the presence of an invisible person with you;

19. A voice always tells you that you cannot marry (sometimes in your thoughts or in your dreams).

Steps to Freedom

You can be free from this evil spiritual bondage. I too was bound by a spirit wife. The torment was too much but Jesus set me free. Today he has used me to deliver so many people. He will set you free too if you will follow these steps:

1. Repent from every sin you have identified.

2. Put away any sexual partner who is not your spouse.

3. Break the soul tie with that person.

4. Destroy any pornographic materials in your keeping.

5. Destroy any idol, charm or occult materials.

6. Prayer and fasting. Pray until you are free.

7. In case you cannot handle it alone, meet a godly deliverance minster for assistance.

Prayers to Break Evil Spiritual Marriages

After you have repented from your sins and decided in your heart to follow Jesus, pray these prayers very AGGRESSIVELY. Do not stop even if there is a strange manifestation in you. After praying these two prayers, continue with the other prayer points.

1. Prayer to cancel every evil spiritual marriage:

I renounce and cancel with the blood of Jesus any evil spiritual marriage, established between me and any evil spirit, consciously or unconsciously, in the name of Jesus. Let any claim the spirit husband/wife has on me be made of no effect by the blood of Jesus Christ. Let any legal ground in the form of an agreement, promises, vows and covenants made on my behalf by whosoever, be canceled by the blood of Jesus Christ, in the name of Jesus. I renounce and reject any marriage ring or any token given to me by that spirit wife/husband in the name of Jesus. I break every rule and law binding me to him/ her with the blood of Jesus. I set on fire any wedding certificate, wedding ring, gown and gifts. Let every spirit child that exists between us be roasted by fire now, in the name of Jesus. Let the blood of Jesus that cleanses from all impurities purge my body, soul and spirit of every sexual pollution and contamination of the spirit husband/ wife, in the name of Jesus.

2. Prayer to break evil marriage covenants:

Every covenant that is binding me to any evil spiritual marriage be broken now, In the mighty name of Jesus! For it is written: "God has made a new covenant with me in the blood of Jesus Christ, and all other covenants are null and powerless". Every curse placed upon my body, my business, my property, my home and my marriage by the sprit husband/wife, loosen your hold over me now, By the blood of Jesus! Who shall curse him that the Lord has blessed? From today I am blessed and no curse shall abide on me again. No evil spirit shall rule my life again, in the mighty name of Jesus.

1. *Every spirit wife/ husband receive fire and be paralyzed and leave me now, in the name of Jesus.*
2. *I command everything you have deposited in my life to come out by fire, in the name of Jesus.*
3. *Every power that is working against my marriage, scatter, in the name of Jesus.*
4. *I divorce and renounce my marriage with the spirit husband or wife, in the name of Jesus.*
5. *I break all covenants entered into with the spirit husband or wife, in the name of Jesus.*
6. *I command the thunder and fire of God to burn to ashes the wedding gown, ring, photographs and all other materials used for the marriage, in Jesus' name.*
7. *I send the fire of God to burn to ashes the marriage certificate, in the name of Jesus.*
8. *I renounce and break every blood and soul-tie covenants with the spirit husband or wife, in the name of Jesus.*
9. *I send thunder and the fire of God to burn to ashes the children born to the marriage, in Jesus' name.*
10. *I withdraw my blood, sperm or any other part of my body deposited on the altar of the spirit husband or wife, in Jesus name.*
11. *You spirit husband or wife tormenting my life and earthly marriage, I bind you with hot chains and fetters of God and cast you out of my life into the deep pit, and I command you not to ever come into my life again, in the name of Jesus.*
12. *I return to you every property of yours in my possession in the spirit world, including the dowry and whatsoever was used for the marriage and covenants, in the name of Jesus.*

13. I drain myself of all evil materials deposited in my body as a result of our sexual relations, in Jesus' name.

14. Lord, send the Holy Ghost fire into my root and burn out all unclean things deposited in it by the spirit husband or wife, in the name of Jesus.

15. I crush the head of any snake, deposited into my body by the spirit husband or wife to do me harm, and command it to come out, in the name of Jesus.

16. I purge out, with the blood of Jesus, every evil material deposited in my womb to prevent me from having children on earth.

17. Lord, repair and restore every damage done to any part of my body and my earthly marriage by the spirit husband or wife, in the name of Jesus.

18. I reject and cancel every curse, evil pronouncement, spell, jinx, enchantment and incantation placed upon me by the spirit husband or wife, in the name of Jesus.

19. I take back and possess all my earthly belongings in the custody of the spirit husband or wife, in Jesus' name.

20. I command the spirit husband or wife to turn his or her back on me forever, in Jesus' name.

21. I renounce and reject the name given to me by the spirit husband or wife, in the name of Jesus.

22. I hereby declare and confess that the Lord Jesus Christ is my Husband for eternity, in Jesus' name.

23. I soak myself in the blood of Jesus and cancel the evil mark or writings placed on me, in Jesus' name.

24. I set myself free from the stronghold, domineering power and bondage of the spirit husband or wife, in the name of Jesus.

25. I paralyze the remote control power and work used to destabilize my earthly marriage, and to hinder me from bearing children for my earthly husband or wife, in the name of Jesus.

26. *I announce to the heavens that I am forever married to Jesus.*

27. *Every trademark of an evil marriage, be shaken out of my life, in the name of Jesus.*

28. *I declare myself a virgin for the Lord, in Jesus' name.*

29. *Let every evil veil upon my life be torn open, in Jesus' name.*

30. *O Lord, restore all marriages that have been destroyed by the spirits of succubus and incubus in the name of Jesus.*

Marriage breakthrough prayers for the unmarried:

1. *Lord, I praise you because you care for me and my destiny is in your hands.*

2. *Ask the Lord to forgive and purge you with the blood Jesus of any sin you know.*

3. *I renounce and cancel with the blood of Jesus any marriage covenant with the kingdom of darkness in Jesus' name.*

4. *I return or cancel any spiritual bride-price paid or received on my behalf in the name of Jesus.*

5. *I command any spiritual marriage certificate binding me with a spirit spouse to catch fire and burn to ashes in the name of Jesus.*

6. *I break every curse brought upon me by inherited sexual sins and also by personal sexual sins in the name of Jesus.*

7. *I renounce and break any anti-marriage covenant made by me or made by someone else on my behalf in the name of Jesus.*

8. *I cancel every anti-marriage spell, bewitchment and incantation on my life in the name of Jesus.*

9. *I break any anti-marriage generational curse over my life in the name of Jesus.*

10. *I take authority and I bind any strongman, from my mother's house or my father's house opposing marriage in my life in the name of Jesus.*

11. *I command any demon opposing marriage in my life to leave me now*

and go in the name of Jesus!

12. I command all anti-marriage satanic spiritual garments and gadgets in my life to catch fire and burn to ashes, in the name of Jesus.

13. I command any evil kingdom fighting against marriage in my life to catch fire and burn to ashes in the name of Jesus.

14. I bind every spirit of fear and anxiety concerning marriage in my life in the name of Jesus.

15. I command any idol, shrine or spiritual prison holding my marital destiny to release it now in the name of Jesus.

16. Anything planted in me to hinder me from getting married, die now!, in the name of Jesus!

17. I command any evil power holding my husband/wife to release him/her in the name of Jesus.

18. Let the power of the Holy Ghost draw my partner to me in the name of Jesus.

19. O Lord, release the angel of marriage to visit me and turn my situation around in the name of Jesus.

20. Today I receive grace and favor from the Lord to marry, in the name of Jesus.

21. I receive grace and strength to wait for the manifestation of this miracle in my life in the name of Jesus.

22. I decree that I will not marry the wrong person in Jesus name.

23. I decree that I shall not fall into any satanic trap concerning marriage in Jesus' name.

24. I receive the anointing to discern God's will concerning marriage in the name of Jesus.

DAYS 21 – 22

TOTAL RECOVERY

"So I will restore to you the years that the swarming locust has eaten, The crawling locust, The consuming locust, And the chewing locust, My great army which I sent among you" (Joel 2:25).

There are certain personal and family blessings that have been lost and which God wants to restore to you on this mountain. He will do this by releasing an anointing of recovery on your life. God released this anointing on the children of Israel when they were about to leave Egypt and within hours they recovered their blessings which for generations the Egyptians had stolen from them.

"Now the children of Israel had done according to the word of Moses, and they had asked from the Egyptians articles of silver, articles of gold, and clothing. And the LORD had given the people favor in the sight of the Egyptians, so that they granted them what they requested. Thus they plundered the Egyptians" (Ex.12:35-36).

The recovery anointing that came on Israel is called in Exodus 12:36 "Favor." God's favour will be activated mightily on your family for unstoppable divine restoration.

Be Determined for Total Recovery

People only go out on risky recovery missions when

they have lost something they consider to be very valuable. I pray that God will open your eyes to see what the devil has stolen from you and your family. Family people who were supposed to be vibrant servants of God by now are still serving at the altars of demons. Some families that should have been reaching out to other families by now are still living at hand to mouth level. Individuals who should be flying in life like eagles are crawling in the dust of failure and stagnation. Somebody must rise up and say, "This nonsense must stop!" Until you arrive at this critical point, you may never break through and break forward into God's best for your life. Isaac said to His son Esau,

"You'll live by your sword, hand-to-mouth, and you'll serve your brother. But when you can't take it any more you'll break loose and run free" (Gen.27:40) M.

When the time came for Israel to be delivered from Egypt, Pharaoh refused to let them go. As Moses and Aaron continued to mount pressure on him, he began to present certain proposals that I want us to examine:

1. Go and sacrifice to your God in the Land (Ex.8:25):

Pharaoh sensed that the Israelites were going out of Egypt for good, so he proposed a plan that would keep them in the land. To remain and serve God in the land meant, they would never become a nation, they would continue to be slaves, and the blessings of the Promised Land would never be theirs. Above all staying in the land was not God's plan for them. That is how Satan operates.

Satan wants to deceive you to think that you can live like the people of the land but still be accepted by God. No! A sinner cannot be a Believer and a Believer cannot be a sinner. The journey of divine recovery will start when you surrender all your sins and turn fully to Jesus Christ.

2. You can go and sacrifice to your God in the wilderness but not very far (Ex.8:28):

Pharaoh knew that to allow Israel to go far was tantamount to losing them. So he told them to go out of the land but not to go too far. The second proposal seemed better than the first one but it was still not God's will. God's word, "Let my people go," meant deliverance, relocation and restoration. Moses and Aaron refused to compromise.

Satan does not want you to go far. He wants you to be a shallow Christian who still keeps some sins. He tells you, "Don't worry, you are better than others, it is ok. Take it easy." In Pidgin they say, "Tekam small small."

How are you serving God? Are you compromising with unbelievers or are you determined to break out of the corrupt worldly system and pursue the kingdom of God and His righteousness? The anointing of recovery can only rest on those who are determined to please God fully.

3. Let only the men go and serve God (Ex.10:11):

What a terrible proposal! Can you imagine that Moses accepted to leave Egypt only with the men, leaving behind all the women and the children? It is clear that after a short time, the people would have returned to Egypt to meet their families.

Is this not a strategy the devil is using today? He has held captive either spouses or children in sin and he is telling parents, "Go ahead and serve your God." How many have finally backslid and returned to sin because their loved ones remained under the rule of Satan. We are going to ask God to intervene in our families for the salvation of our loved ones who are still bound by Satan. Arise and declare to the devil like Moses,

"We will go with our young and our old; with our sons and our daughters, with our flocks and our herds we will go, for we must hold a feast to the LORD" (Ex.10:9).

In other words, "My family will not remain under the rule of Satan; they must serve the living God whom I serve, in the name of Jesus."

4. Go and serve the Lord with your families but leave behind your flocks (Ex.10:24):

Pharaoh was saying "Go and serve your God empty handed." How on earth do you go to serve God without your wealth?

Moses responded,

"You must allow us to have sacrifices and burnt offerings to present to the Lord our God" (Ex.10:25).

I love the way Moses puts it; "YOU MUST." Moses reminded Pharaoh firmly that they needed their animals to sacrifice to God. God is going to restore you economically so that you can use your wealth to serve Him. Moses further added that,

"Our livestock too <u>must go with us;</u> not a hoof is to be left behind. We have to use some of them in worshiping the Lord our God, and until we get there we will not know what we are to use to worship the Lord" NIV.

They were determined to leave Egypt with all that God had given them.

Disarming God's children economically is a satanic

strategy to fight the advancement of the gospel. Beloved in the Lord, we cannot allow the kingdom of darkness and their agents sit on our God-given blessings when we go after God empty handed. Whatever belongs to us and our children must come back to us. Satan wants us to be poor and miserable so as to frustrate God's purposes for our lives. We say no to that, in Jesus' name. The power of Pharaoh sitting over our economy must break, in the mighty name of Jesus.

Let us believe God for spiritual and economic recovery as we pray this season. Pray that spiritual gifts and virtues that have been lost in our lives be restored. Also pray that the fortunes of families and of our nation be fully restored.

1st Day: PRAYER POINTS

1. *Take time and worship God for bringing you to this special season of divine recovery.*
2. *Thank God because He is going to restore lost blessings to your life and family.*
3. *O Lord, in the name of Jesus forgive me for any carelessness that has given the devil the opportunity to steal from me.*
4. *Lord, forgive me for mismanaging the resources you gave me in the name of Jesus.*
5. *Lord, forgive me for following the evil and sinful ways of my parents, in the name of Jesus.*
6. *Lord, forgive my church and community for opening up to demons through sin.*
7. *O Lord God of mercy, have mercy upon us and release the river of restoration to heal us and our land, in the name of Jesus.*
8. *O Lord, release the fire of the Holy Ghost upon us for total recovery*

in our lives and families, in the name of Jesus.

9. Father, put a passion in our hearts and cause us not to rest until we become what you want us to be in Christ Jesus, in the name of Jesus.

10. Lord, open our eyes to discover our divine inheritance, as well as the stolen blessings of our family, in the name of Jesus.

11. Lord, open the eyes of church leaders to discover the blessings that the devil has stolen from the church, in the name of Jesus.

12. In the mighty name of Jesus, I stand today on the finished work of the cross and I cancel with the blood of Jesus any covenant established by my fore-fathers with evil spirits that mortgaged the blessings of my family.

13. In the mighty name of Jesus, I cancel any satanic record that gives evil spirits the right to hold my family's blessings, in the name of Jesus.

14. In the mighty name of Jesus, I use the blood of Jesus to cancel any satanic legal ground that permits the devil to oppress our church, in the name of Jesus.

15. In the mighty name of Jesus, I use the blood of Jesus to cancel any satanic legal ground that permits the devil to imprison the blessings of our nation, in the name of Jesus.

16. I bind any spiritual strongman responsible for keeping me and my family away from our blessings, in the name of Jesus.

17. I command any demonic power sitting over my divine inheritance to scatter by fire, in the name of Jesus.

18. In the mighty name of Jesus, I command all the forces of darkness sitting over the blessings of my tribe to scatter by fire.

19. In the mighty name of Jesus, I command all the forces of darkness manipulating the blessings of this nation to scatter by fire.

20. O Lord, let your east wind blow through my life, family, church and nation for a mighty breakthrough, in the mighty name of Jesus.

21. My Father, let the river of divine restoration bring salvation,

healing, deliverance and breakthrough into my life, family, church and nation, in the name of Jesus.

22. *Lord, raise anointed men and women in each family in this nation, in the name of Jesus.*

2nd *Day: PRAYER POINTS*

1. *Take time and worship God for bringing you to this special season of divine recovery.*

2. *Thank God because He is going to restore lost blessings to your life.*

3. *O Lord, forgive me for any carelessness that has given the devil the opportunity to steal from me, in the name of Jesus.*

4. *Lord, thank you because you will restore …….. (Name it) that the devil has stolen, in the name of Jesus.*

5. *I command any satanic army that has taken captive ……… (Mention names) to scatter to pieces in the name of Jesus.*

6. *O Mighty God of King David, send the angels of divine recovery into my life, family and church for miraculous recovery of lost generational blessings, in the name of Jesus.*

7. *O Lord, let the anointing of resurrection cause every dead thing in my life and family to come back to life.*

8. *My Father, release the anointing of divine attraction to bring back all I have lost, in the name of Jesus.*

9. *O Lord, let the anointing of divine acceleration fall on me today for total recovery, in the name of Jesus.*

10. *My Father, let doors of restoration, salvation, healing, provision, favor, promotion and fruitfulness open in my life, family, church and this nation, in the name of Jesus.*

11. *O Lord, cause your wind to blow through my life and cause the good in me to manifest.*

12. *O Lord, let your fire burn every veil that has caused darkness to*

prevail over any area of my life, in the name of Jesus.

13. My Father, let your east wind blow through my family and expose every evil that has been ruining us, in the name of Jesus.

14. O God of mercy, let there be total recovery of everything the devil has stolen from me and my family (Identify the different areas).

15. My Father, according to your word, give me seven fold recovery in this area of my life .... (Name it), in the name of Jesus.

16. O God of revival, let lost spiritual gifts, anointing, evangelism, giving, fasting, love and faith be restored in the churches in this nation, in the name of Jesus.

17. O Lord, let your east wind blow through my life, family, church and nation for a mighty spiritual and economic breakthrough.

18. My Father, let the river of divine restoration bring salvation, healing, deliverance and breakthrough into my life, family, church and nation, in the name of Jesus.

19. O Lord, cause my family to see miracles we have never seen before, in the name of Jesus.

20. Let the power of Pharaoh sitting on the economy of this nation break, in the name of Jesus.

DAY 23

PRAYER FOR MISSIONS AND MISSIONARIES

Use the prayer topics on Day 18.

DAY 24

BUILD A FAMILY ALTAR

Altars have a lot to do in the restoration of a family. It is on the altar that God's fire for deliverance, healing and restoration will fall. Wherever an altar of pure worship to the living God is broken, the result is spiritual famine and demonic harassments. In 1Kings 17 and 18, we see how the nation of Israel went through a three and a half year period of harsh famine and pain because they had abandoned God's altar and raised evil altars to Baal. As long as the altars of Baal were standing, the whole nation was plunged into spiritual darkness. The heavens over them were sealed, the potentials of individuals were thwarted and wickedness became rampant in the land. When Elijah came onto the scene, the first thing he did was that he repaired God's broken altar (1kgs.18:30-39). He went on and asked for the manifestation of God's glory. Within a few minutes, fire fell from heaven and consumed the sacrifice, together with the 12 stones of the altar. Rain fell that day and the restoration of Israel began. Baalism began to crumble in Israel.

This is the reason why I have to show you how to raise a family altar for God. When pure worship shall begin to go up to God from your father's house, deliverance, healing and restoration shall become a reality in your family. Your mourning shall turn to dancing and your shame shall be turned to double honor (Isa.61:1-7).

What is a Family Altar?

A family altar is the place where members of a household gather to worship God, study the word of God and also present their prayer requests to Him. Many other spiritual activities take place at the family altar, like fasting, teaching, laying on of hands for impartation, rebuke, instruction, counseling, etc.

The Family altar in a nuclear family:

This is the family altar of a husband, wife and children. Each household should have this type of family altar. Some families have their family altar in their sitting room while others have a special room set aside in the family house for prayers. Families practice the family altar in different ways. Some families meet at the family altar twice a day – early in the morning before they go out and in the evening before they go to bed. Others meet every morning, while others meet on some days of the week.

The extended family altar:

This altar is a place where the extended family meets to worship and seek the face of God. The extended family in this sense speaks of parents, children and their wives, grandchildren, cousins etc. (People of the same blood line). In our communities we have what people call "Family meetings." The family meetings bring together members of the nuclear family as well as other relatives. Sometimes the family altar of the nuclear family grows into the extended family altar. When we were young, we used to gather in our sitting room to pray as a family but today that we are all grown up and married with our wives and children, we all meet together once a year to worship God.

So instead of just meeting to discuss issues of family development, worshipping and honoring God should become the center of it. You should plan to meet with God as a family at least once a year.

How to run an extended family altar:

1. You need a spiritual leader:
This is the person who should direct the spiritual activities of the altar. There is never an altar without a priest to service it. The person who will serve as the spiritual leader must be someone who has a living relationship with God. That is someone who is anointed by the Holy Spirit. The person can be the family head or any other family member. The leader can be a man or a woman. Pray that God should raise a spiritual leader for your family.

2. You need a program:
The spiritual leader should bring the family members together to agree on a program. The program should include:

a. *Date of meeting.* At least once a year.
b. *The place of meeting.* It can be in the family house or you could agree to rotate the meetings. In my family we meet alternately in the homes of different family members once a year.
c. *Organize a family month or family week yearly.* This is a program to wait on God on behalf of the family. All family members forward their prayer topics to the spiritual leader for the establishment of a prayer guide. When all the prayer points are put together,

the leader shares them to all the members. On the guide the details on how the prayer program will run are indicated. For example when the family should fast and when they should meet together to pray. I encourage you to plan your family week or family month prior to the general meeting, so that you meet to carry out the program together.

d. *Intense prayer.* Your family meeting should include a time of intense prayer for the family.

e. *Invite a servant of God.* Invite anointed servants of God to minister to you when you meet as a family. They will teach and guide you in the ways of God. If you are blessed to have God's servants in your family like we do in mine then it is wonderful.

f. *Break curses.* Break any curse that is identified in the family at your family altar. There are situations that bow when you address them with one voice.

g. *Parental blessing.* The head of the family should pronounce blessings on the family. I gave some scriptures earlier that can help you to pray blessings on your family. My father lays hands on all of us once a year to bless us.

h. *Support one another.* Pray for divine intervention in the life of one another. Also support each other financially or materially.

i. *Present a sacrifice.* When families that worship idols meet they raise offerings to buy animals to present sacrifices to their ancestors and their gods. When children of God meet as a family they should collect a special offering to present to God. This will activate God's blessings on the family. Whenever we meet as a family, we raise a free will offering to present to God. Each one of us together with our wives and children give as God has blessed us. In the past we used to give the money to pastors and ask them to pray for our family. When the amount became reasonable, we give part of it to orphans and widows.

A few questions and answers:

1. What if you are the only believer in your family?
A. Follow the program I have proposed above alone. Believe God for the salvation of other family members. God will begin to save them. There was a time when my mother was the only believer in the family, but today she is no longer alone. Her husband, children, sisters, brothers, etc, have come to the Lord and some are even pastors.

2. Just few of us are believers, what do we do?
A. The few who are believers should start to meet and seek God for a visitation in the family. Follow the program I have proposed above. You can meet in the family house and pray.

3. What if the family head is against our spiritual activities?
A. Those who are believers should work together. Pray for your family head. Never see him as an enemy. One day the persecutor will join you.

4. A few family members are against us. What do we do?
Work with those who have caught the vision but always inform those who are against it when you have to pray as a

family. Never sideline them and consider them your enemies. Fight against the spirit of division in your family.

Build your Family Altar

It is commonly said that "The family that prays together stays together." This saying is true. When we meet as a family there is a level of anointing released that can never be experienced when we are alone.

"Behold, how good and how pleasant it is for brethren to dwell together in unity! It is like the precious ointment upon the head, that ran down upon the beard, even Aaron's beard: that went down to the skirts of his garments; As the dew of Hermon, and as the dew that descended upon the mountains of Zion: for there the LORD commanded the blessing, even life for evermore" (Ps.133:1-3).

The devil being conscious of this has vowed to tear families apart. He does this by first attacking the family altar. He ensures that family members should not meet to pray. Some families actually operate under the principle of "Everyone for himself, God for all us." People live in some family houses like students in a public boarding house. Every morning they wake up at different times. While some pray, some go to look for something to eat and leave for their daily activities. In the evening each individual retires to bed when they are tired of watching TV. The family scarcely has a time to sit before God. Some children are demonized; others are involved in terrible cults, but the parents do not know. How do you expect such a family to grow in the fear of God?

Some people pray with their spouses and their children but do not care about what is going on in the families of their brothers, sisters and other relatives. They attend family meetings but they say nothing about raising an altar for God. Some believers out of fear and shame will not even request to pray when they meet in the family compound for meetings. How do you expect light to shine in your family?

When your family altar is on fire, God's presence keeps your family from trouble. The Lord says,

"For I,' says the LORD, 'will be a wall of fire all around her, and I will be the glory in her midst" (Zec.2:5).

Now that you know the importance of the family altar, decide to raise one if you have never had it. If yours has been broken down, rebuild it today. Some people in your house may not like it. Let that not stop you. As the fire begins to grow they will join you. Do everything to raise a family altar in your family.

PRAYER POINTS

Take time and praise God for the gift of family. If you have family members around who are following this program with you, pray these prayers together.

1. *Ask the Holy Spirit for grace and power to pray till you experience family breakthrough.*
2. *Ask God to forgive you and your family members for neglecting God's altar.*
3. *O Lord, we surrender any strange altar we have raised in our family consciously or unconsciously and we ask your fire to consume it to ashes in the name of Jesus.*
4. *I dedicate my life and my entire family to you today for a work of restoration in the name of Jesus.*
5. *Now pray and ask God to lead you on how to raise a family altar*

in your family.

6. *Take time now and come out with a clear plan of action.*

7. *Present your plan to the Lord and ask Him to help you realize it before you continue to pray.*

8. *Every evil hand assigned to scatter my family, I command that hand to wither in the name of Jesus.*

9. *Every ancestral altar speaking against my family, catch fire and burn to ashes in the name of Jesus Christ.*

10. *I command every tree of confusion in my house to be uprooted in the name of Jesus.*

11. *Pray aggressively against the following spirits as follows:*

12. *I stand against the spirit of . . . and I command you to pack out of my family in the name of Jesus.*

   a. *spirit of division*
   b. *spirit of spiritual slumber*
   c. *spirit of rebellion against the word of God*
   d. *spirit of religion*
   e. *spirit of manipulation*
   f. *anti-prayer spirit*
   g. *spirit of divorce*
   h. *familiar and ancestral spirits*
   i. *spirit of household destruction*
   j. *spirit of fear*
   k. *spirit of misunderstanding*
   l. *spirit of destruction*

13. *Any power conspiring with anyone to destroy my family, be scattered in the name of Jesus.*

14. *O Lord, release the spirit of revelation and the fear of God upon my family members in the name of Jesus.*

15. *Let every stronghold of the enemy barricading the minds of my family members from receiving Jesus be pulled down in the*

name of Jesus. (Mention names).

16. I bind any demonic strong man assigned against my family to hinder us from experiencing God's blessings ordained for us, in the name of Jesus.

17. In the name of Jesus, I break any curse operating on my family and hindering us from making progress.

18. I bind and cast away from my family members every spirit of spiritual blindness in the name of Jesus.

19. O Lord, open the eyes of my family members and cause them to become restless until they come to Jesus.

20. O Lord, let your divine word come powerfully to all my family members in the name of Jesus.

21. In the mighty name of Jesus, I commit myself to raise an altar of pure worship in my family.

22. O Lord, let the altar of pure worship in my family never collapse in the name of Jesus.

23. I pull down every stronghold of oppression in my family in the name of Jesus.

24. I decree my release and the release of all the members of my household from any form of oppression in the name of Jesus.

25. I declare today in the mighty name of Jesus, yoke of oppression over my family, break to pieces.

26. .Every ancestral oppression working in my family, break completely in the name of Jesus.

27. In the mighty name of Jesus, I trample upon any serpent and scorpion that is oppressing my family.

28. Every witchcraft and occult oppression, be neutralized in the name of Jesus.

29. Every power of oppression working against any area of my family, die in the name of Jesus.

30. Let the fire of divine judgment melt every chain and yoke of

oppression working against my life.

31. *Father let the anointing for total spiritual expansion overflow in my life in the name of Jesus.*

DAY 25

O LORD, SEND US REVIVAL

Use the prayer points on Day 4.

RAISING PILLARS IN THE FAMILY

Any family that is vibrant is standing on a solid foundation and supported by strong pillars. Families fall apart because of broken foundations and the absence of strong pillars.

A Strong Family Foundation

The foundation of the family can be summarized into two aspects:

1. The parents:

Parents transfer a lot to their children both genetically and spiritually. I am black because my ancestors were black people. I have had to fight some spiritual battles not because I did anything wrong but because of my ancestry.

There are also virtues that flow from the parents to children. God uses parents unconsciously to lay strong genetic foundations for their children. For example, many of us are very musical and artistic. We also see these virtues evident in our parents. So we do not just pass on negative traits to our children. There are hidden treasures in us that we have inherited from our parents. You have to identify these treasures and begin to exploit them. On the 1st of August 2015, a book titled *"Swimming to Success"* was launched in Texas – USA. It was written by my younger brother's daughter who is ten years old. She is the fifth in our family to publish a book. Her father is a writer too. Each family has those powerful genes.

2. The value system:

The next foundation stone for a strong family is what I call "The value system." This speaks of what you believe is right or wrong. For example: respect for elders, the fear of God, keeping yourself sexually pure, respect for state property, etc. When you can successfully inculcate the right value systems in the children, then you have laid a strong foundation for your family.

The tool God has given to use for the building of our families is His word. How many families in this nation have chosen to build their lives on this divine word? Unfortunately many children grow up without the knowledge of God's principles because their parents have rejected the word of God. How do you expect your family to stand strong against the storms of life when God is absent? In Mathew 7:24-27, Jesus Christ revealed that the word of God is the bedrock upon which a strong house (A family) should be built.

"Therefore whoever hears these sayings of Mine, and does them, I will liken him to a wise man who built his house [family] on the rock."

Strong Pillars for your Family

The pillars of the family are the family members God has raised to provide the support that the family needs. Each family needs a governor, a guide and a guard. When a family has people operating at these three levels, there is stability and progress. Any family that is not making meaningful progress lacks these three basic pillars. May God raise yours, in Jesus' name.

We are going to use three Bible characters to illustrate what I mean:

1. Samuel:

Samuel was a prophet and priest whom God raised for the restoration of Israel (1sam.3). As a priest, he taught them the ways of God. He also interceded for them in times of trouble (1Sam.7). As a prophet, he provided prophetic direction for them (1Sam.12). Under his leadership Israel's hand was heavy on her enemies.

Each family needs a "Samuel," who will teach them the ways of God and also give them prophetic direction. You do not need a soothsayer but someone who can guide you prophetically to walk in the ways of God.

2. A David:

David was a king and a warrior who fought battles to establish Israel in their divine inheritance. It was under his rule that Israel occupied the whole land that God had given to Israel (1Chron.18:3). It was David who killed the giant Goliath who stood against Israel (1Sam.17).

You need a "David" in your family who will govern the people with the fear of God. You need one with the kingly anointing who will judge the forces of darkness that have been oppressing your family. The Goliath of your family will fall when such a one is raised. You need an anointed of the Lord who will lead you to fight the Lord's battles in your family for the deliverance of your divine inheritance.

3. A Joseph:

Joseph was a young man whom God raised to become the bread winner for the nation of Israel. God positioned him spiritually, politically and economically to meet the needs of Israel (Ps.105:16-24). He was their god-father, their senator and their parliamentarian. God used Joseph to raise a great nation in a strange land.

You need a Joseph in your family who will contribute to establish family members.

We are going to pray fervently because we know that it is going to take God to raise this caliber of anointed servants in our families. God has actually raised some of these instruments in some families already, but they have not yet discovered their divine assignments. God will open their eyes as we pray. In other families, individuals refuse to submit to the authority of the leaders. This creates unnecessary frictions. Deal with this.

Let me talk to somebody who has been established by God but who has abandoned his/her family. Please I know that you have tangible reasons why you have closed up to them. Consider the story of Joseph (Gen.37 – 47). Despite the evil that his brothers did to him, he still went on and took good care of them. Allow God to judge. See yourself as their bread winner. Give them the bread to eat. Why should they perish when you are there? Send their children to school. Build a house for them. Do your best to improve on their wellbeing. God will bless you and your children.

PRAYER POINTS

1. *Lord, thank you for the gift of my family.*
2. *O Lord, thank you making me a member in this special family, in the name of Jesus.*
3. *Father, thank you for the pillars you are raising in my family, in the name of Jesus.*

4. *Appreciate God for every family member and for the gifts of God in their lives (Mention their name).*

5. *Father, help each member of my family to discover their gifts and give them grace to develop them.*

6. *O Lord, let our destinies open up, in the name of Jesus.*

7. *I bind any power assigned to cut off our virtues, in the name of Jesus.*

8. *I pull down the stronghold of stagnation in my family, in the name of Jesus.*

9. *Father, raise and anoint Samuels in my family who will teach us your ways and guide us to fulfill our destinies, in the name of Jesus.*

10. *Let the door of salvation open for my family and let the word of God grow mightily among us, in the name of Jesus.*

11. *Father, let your righteous right hand cut down any power that fights your word in my family, in the name of Jesus.*

12. *O Lord, raise Davids with the kingly anointing, who will lead us to fight the Lord's battles, in the name of Jesus.*

13. *Lord, anoint sons and daughters of my father's house and of my mother's house who will cut off the heads of our goliaths, in the name of Jesus.*

14. *Lord, raise and anoint Josephs who will eradicate lack and misery from our family, in the name of Jesus.*

15. *My Father, turn around our captivity in this season, in the name of Jesus.*

16. *Now identify the different areas of your family that need restoration and begin to ask God to bring change.*

17. *Present the needs of different family members to the Lord.*

18. *Take time pray for a turnaround in specific areas of your family.*

DAY 27

COVENANT DAY OF HEALING

"Bless the LORD, O my soul, And forget not all His benefits: Who forgives all your iniquities, Who heals all your diseases" (Ps.103:2-3).

Today we are going to engage the covenant of healing God has established with us in the blood of Jesus Christ against all diseases and infirmities that have been tormenting you. I believe that as we pray today the Lord our God who is merciful, compassionate and all powerful will heal you in Jesus' name. Today Jesus Christ our great physician will be walking among us on this Mountain of Restoration to heal all manner of diseases. Get ready for your miracle! I release healing and deliverance angels now to begin to minister to you, in Jesus' name.

What is the Covenant of Healing?
The healing covenant speaks first of **God's promise to heal** His children who are sick. Secondly it speaks of **God's provision for your healing** which is the blood of Jesus Christ shed on the cross. The Bible declares boldly that,
"By His stripes you were healed" (1Pet.2:24).
And thirdly, the healing covenant speaks of **your right to be healed** by the power of God. God's healing covenant name is *"Jehovah Rapha"* – The LORD who heals (Ex.15:26).
"If you diligently heed the voice of the LORD your God and do what is right in His sight, give ear to His commandments and keep all His statutes, I will put

none of the diseases on you which I have brought on the Egyptians. For I am the LORD who heals you."

A covenant is usually a mutual understanding between two or more parties, each binding himself to fulfill specified obligations. In the healing covenant deal, God has committed Himself **to heal** and **to spare** His covenant children from diseases. So it is all about God healing you when you are sick and also keeping you immune to sicknesses and diseases (Divine health). On the other hand, the beneficiaries of the covenant *must keep all His commandments*. By this covenant God became a medical doctor for the Israelites as they went through the harsh wilderness. Hear the result;

"He also brought them out ... And there was none feeble among His tribes" (Ps.105:37).

He too can become your doctor as you affiliate to the covenant through Jesus Christ. He will heal you and preserve you in good health.

Why Sicknesses and Diseases?

Sicknesses did not come until after the fall of man in Genesis chapter 3. Sin is actually the foundation of all sicknesses and diseases. A study of Psalm 103:1-5 reveals that there are about five different sources of sickness. In each case God reveals to us a solution.

1. Sin (Ps.103:3):

Diseases come because of sin. Whenever you break God's commandments you open the gates of your life to spirits of infirmity and affliction. Ecclesiastes 10:8 illustrates it in this way,

"He who digs a pit will fall into it, And whoever breaks through a wall will be bitten by a serpent."

Digging the pit or breaking the wall speaks of committing sin. The serpent speaks of spirits of destruction that afflict the sinner.

God's provision to deal with diseases that have come through sin is forgiveness. He can forgive all your sins if you are ready to confess and abandon them. Remember the case of the desperate paralytic man who was brought to Jesus in Mathew 9:1-8. The first thing Jesus did was that He forgave the man's sins. After dealing with the sin that was the root cause of the problem, the man received his healing instantly.

Examine your life now. If there is any sin you know of that can be the cause of your sickness, kneel down and ask God to forgive you, in Jesus' name. Also carry out restitution where it is needed. If you do not know of any sin that you need to confess, just cast your whole life at the Master's feet. Tell Him to expose anything that may be hidden in your life.

2. Demonic attacks (Ps.103:4):

Most of the diseases afflicting people are caused by evil spirits. You find people who are very sick and dying but cannot be helped medically. In most cases it is impossible to diagnose the cause of the problem.

If you have such a health situation that has defied all medical assistance do not give up. In the healing covenant God has made provision for your healing and restoration. Psalm 103:4 says, *"Who redeems your life from destruction."* Your healing will come by the deliverance power in the covenant. Many times Jesus Christ healed different kinds of diseases by casting out demons.

The above verse speaks about redemption. To redeem means to pay the price for the liberation of a slave. The price for your redemption from the slave market of sickness was paid more than two thousand years ago. That price is the blood of Jesus Christ that was shed (Eph.1:7). Satan has no right any longer to hold you captive with sickness

Just get ready, the anointing that breaks yokes and bondages is going to manifest in your life now. Open your heart and welcome God's healing power into your life now.

"I bind and cast out of your life that spirit of infirmity, in the mighty name of Jesus Christ. Let every rope or chain of sickness holding you down in sickness burn to ashes by the fire of the Holy Ghost, in Jesus' name." Lay your hand on your head and declare seven times, *"Let any chain of sickness in my life, catch fire now and burn, in Jesus name."* After declaring seven times, close your eyes and take a deep breath for five seconds then breathe out fast. Do that seven *times.* Declare seven times, *"I am free, in Jesus' name."*

In case there is a strange manifestation, do not stop, continue until you feel liberated.

3. Emotional breakdown (Ps.103:4):

Emotional breakdowns are responsible for many health problems. The human psychology and physiology always have a direct effect on each other. This means that the state of your mind affects the functioning of your body. For instance if you want to cause someone to become sick in the body, just release depressive thoughts into his mind. You used to hear people say after receiving some bad news, "I am sick about this." You can actually fall seriously sick and even die by receiving and allowing negative words and images to stay for long in your mind. Ralph Waldo Emerson who was said to have been the wisest American who ever lived said,

"A man is what he thinks about all day long." Your thoughts can generate energy for good health, or poison for your destruction.

Satan seeks to clothe people with the garment of mourning and crying. He does this by singing the song, "You will die," in their minds. This enemy of your health called Satan will keep reminding you of someone who had a similar case like yours and died in pains. He will paint pictures of death in your mind and in your dreams. Through counseling I have discovered that many persons who are HIV positive or have some terminal diseases always complain about seeing coffins, graves and dead people in their dreams. The root cause of this is fear. Whenever you accommodate thoughts of hopelessness in your spirit, your dreams become death. Your dreams are seeds of your daily thoughts. Depressed people always have nightmares.

God has provided a Healing Balm for the healing and restoration of your emotions (soul). It is His LOVE and tender MERCIES. David said,

"He crowns me with love and tender mercies" (Ps.103:4b) NLT.

The Amplified says, **"Who redeems your life from the pit and corruption, Who beautifies, dignifies, and crowns you with loving-kindness and tender mercy."**

Good News Says, **"He keeps me from the grave and blesses me with love and mercy."**

For you to experience this restoration power that will uplift your spirit from any pit of depression and clothe you with beauty and color, first reject bitterness, hatred, self-condemnation, anger, anxiety, etc. Hand over to God anything in your life that you cannot change by your own power.

Get ready for the anointing of God that heals and restores the soul. As this anointing moves mightily upon you now, let deep wounds and emotional diseases in your life be healed, in Jesus' name. Lay your hand on your heart and pray, *"Father, thank you because you love me with an everlasting love. Right now, I surrender to your care all conditions in my life that I cannot change. I reject all bitterness, anger, self-condemnation, blame, anxiety, from my heart, in Jesus' name. Right now, I bind and cast out of my life any spirit of anger, bitterness, depression, fear, unbelief, doubt, confusion, self-condemnation, in Jesus' name. I jump out of any pit of depression, fear and frustration now, In Jesus' name!*

I now accept the love and mercies of God over my whole life. I welcome God's anointing for total restoration in my body, soul and spirit, in Jesus' name.

Pray in tongues if you can for about 10 minutes before you continue.

4. Poor feeding habits (Ps.103:5):

People also fall sick and even die because of poor feeding habits. What you eat and drink contributes immensely to either build your body up or destroy it. Do you know that if the devil and all his demons, including all the witches and wizards were bound and sent to hell, some people would still get sick and die? This is because they abuse their bodies through poor eating and drinking habits. If you smoke tobacco and drink alcohol, you do not need the devil to kill you; cancer will destroy you with time.

After listening to lectures on nutrition and healthy eating habits, I began to wonder why our society spends more money training people to treat diseases rather than investing on prevention. If the governments of the nations were to close down all the factories that produce toxic substances that end up in our bodies, most of the diseases people are dying from would disappear. The philosophy of the Bible is "Prevention is far better than cure." But in a capitalistic society that is dominated by self-interest, people only think about how much money they can make and not what happens to those who consume the harmful products.

God's solution to this dilemma according to David in Psalm 103:5 is, satisfying your mouth with good things. Good News says, *"He fills my life with good things, so that I stay young and strong like an eagle."* Can God feed you with tobacco, alcohol and drugs? The answer is NO. So learn to ask yourself this question before you eat and drink, "Can Jesus Christ eat or drink this thing?" Consider what you eat. If you fail to control your mouth, you will accelerate your exit from this life.

Before you go on to pray violently against sickness and the devil, ask yourself whether your eating habits are correct. You are not bound to eat everything. As long as you continue to abuse your body through poor eating habits, no prayer can help you. For some people their deliverance and restoration is in their mouth. They have to regulate their appetites and their health will be ok.

5. Old age (Ps.103:5):

The human body wears out with age. Unfortunately, some people ignore this. When you do so, you start looking for a scape goat to blame for your health challenges and usually the devil falls victim. I watched the mighty Evangelist Billy Graham preaching on a wheel chair at the age of 92 years, looking very fragile. In the days of his youth, he would vibrate on the podium as he delivered his evangelistic sermons with a lot of passion but at 92, he could not even stand. It may be his legs and his back ached. That is old age and not the devil. We have people who naively think that you can always be as strong as when you were very young. Even God does not think like that. He knows that age plays down on the human being he created. That is why He made provision in the healing covenant to handle that.

Psalm 103:5 reveals that God renews those who are wearing out because of age, just as the eagle is renewed.

"Who satisfies your mouth with good things, So that your youth is renewed like the eagle's."

God's Word Translation says, *"The one who fills your life with blessings so that you become young again like an eagle."*

God's power in the healing covenant can service every organ in your body so that, *"You can become young again like an eagle."* So your eyes that are growing dim can be renewed. Your worn out bones can be repaired and revamped.

If you are old and tired, today is the day of renewal. Ask God to breathe freshness on you. Believe God that new strength will begin to ooze out of you. You will be an old man/woman with a difference.

How to Receive your Healing
1. Believe:
Believe that God wants to heal you. Believe that sickness is from the devil and not from God. We have seen the different causes of sickness above. We did not mention God as one of them. Never accuse God of causing you to be sick.

Also believe that divine healing is one of the blessings of salvation that God has made available for you in Jesus Christ. If you have accepted Jesus Christ as your personal Lord and Savior, then it is your right to be healed of any type of disease that the devil is using to torment you. That is why I believe that God is going to heal you of that disease today.

2. Ask God to heal you:

God cannot force any blessing on you. Open your mouth and ask Him to heal and restore you.

3. Receive your healing now by faith:

As you ask, believe that He has heard you and has given you the healing as promised. God cannot lie. Release your faith and grab it. If you refuse to release your faith to grab it, you will never have it. The time is now and not tomorrow. The Bible says,

"In an acceptable time I have heard you, And in the day of salvation I have helped you." Behold, now is the accepted time; behold, now is the day of salvation" (2Cor.6:2).

God is saying the miracle is now, why postpone it? This is the time you have been waiting for. Receive your healing now, in Jesus' name.

Many people have not received their healing because of ignorance. That is why I am taking the pains to explain a few biblical truths concerning divine healing before we begin to pray.

4. Act your faith:

Faith without action is dead (Ja.2:18). If your faith is not accompanied by acts of faith, then that faith is fake. Look at all those who received healing miracles from Jesus Christ. There was a word of faith from Jesus the healer and a corresponding act of faith from the receiver. He told the man at Bethesda, "Rise up, pick up your mat and go" (John 5). The man did not argue, he rose up and was healed.

This is what we call, "The violence of faith." It has to do with you taking an aggressive step to obey the word of the Lord, irrespective of how you feel and what is happening. You must act on God's word to see the manifestation of His power. Sometimes people are healed but they refuse to act on their faith.

As you are reading this message, you feel God's anointing moving in your life. You hear the voice of the Holy Spirit telling you that what the man of God is saying is true. *Now receive your miracle in Jesus' name. "I command that disease in your body to die now, in the name of Jesus. I command any spirit responsible for pain and disease in your body to come out now, In the name of Jesus! I command dead organs to receive new life, in the name of Jesus. Receive new spare parts, in the name of Jesus. Let your bones, nerves, and all sick organs in your body, from you head to your feet be healed now, In the name of Jesus! I command you to vomit out anything in your body that is not planted by God. Come out! Come out now, in Jesus' name! I feel God's power moving all over your body right now."* Begin to do something that you could not do before, in Jesus' name.

Maintain your healing by living a holy life. Respect good eating habits. Exercise regularly.

PRAYER POINTS

(Lay your hand on your body and on those who are sick and pray these prayers fervently)

1. Lord, thank you for your healing power made available for me on the cross.

2. Lord, thank you because I know now that it is your will that I should be healed and also live a healthy life.

3. On the grounds of the finished work of the cross I curse every disease in my body now, In the name of Jesus!

4. I command every spirit of infirmity behind this disease to leave my life now In the name of Jesus!

5. I receive my total healing from ..... (Name the problem) now, In the name of Jesus!

6. I overthrow the citadel of sickness, weakness and fear in my life, in the name of Jesus.

7. I receive the Blood of the Lord Jesus Christ for divine purification, in Jesus' name.

8. I vomit every satanic deposit in my body in the mighty name of Jesus. (If you feel as to vomit, do so).

9. Let the blood, the fire and the living waters of the Most High God wash my system clean from

   - Unprofitable growth in the womb
   - Evil plantations
     - Evil deposits from a spirit husband
     - Impurities acquired from parental contaminations
     - Evil spiritual consumption
     - Hidden sicknesses
     - Remote controlled mechanisms
     - Physical and spiritual incisions
     - Satanic poisons
     - Evil stamps, labels and links, in the name of Jesus.

10. *Let every area of my life become too hot for any evil to inhabit again, in the name of Jesus.*

11. *Let every evil growth in my life be uprooted now, In the name of Jesus!*

12. *Let my body reject every evil inhabitation, in the mighty name of Jesus.*

13. *I pass out any satanic deposit in my intestines, in the name of Jesus.*

14. *I pass out any satanic deposit in my reproductive organs, in the name of Jesus.*

15. *I pass out any satanic deposit in my womb, in the name of Jesus.*

16. *In the name of Jesus, I declare before all the forces of darkness that Jesus Christ is Lord, over every department of my life.*

17. *You foreign hand laid on my womb, release me, in the name of Jesus.*

18. *In the name of Jesus, I break and loose myself from all evil curses, chains, spells, jinxes, bewitchment, witchcraft, and sorcery, which may have been put upon me.*

19. *Let a creative miracle take place in my body, my womb and reproductive system in the name of Jesus.*

20. *Father I ask you in the name of Jesus to send out your medical angels to operate on any area of my body that needs an operation, in the name of Jesus.*

21. *Jehovah Rapha, repair and mend every broken area of my entire life, in the name of Jesus.*

22. *Dear Lord Jesus, from today, become my personal physician.*

23. *O Lord, establish a wall of fire around my life and my family against diseases, in the name of Jesus.*

24. *O Lord, cause your covenant children to enjoy divine health in an outstanding way this year, in the name of Jesus.*

25. *O Lord, restore the gifts of divine healing in the church in the name of Jesus.*

DAYS 28 – 29

COVENANT BLESSINGS

"I will make you a great nation; I will bless you And make your name great; And you shall be a blessing. I will bless those who bless you, And I will curse him who curses you; And in you all the families of the earth shall be blessed" (Gen.12:2-3).

Covenant blessings:

Today and tomorrow are days of the release of covenant blessings. I have discovered that in order to receive divine blessings one must be deliberate. Some people erroneously think that since God is gracious His blessings can flow anyhow. It is true that all of us benefit from God's "Common grace" which includes sunshine, rainfall, the air we breathe, etc. (Mat.5:43-48). But not everybody enjoys God's special blessings. Many scriptures in the Bible reveal to us God's covenant blessings which are reserved for the righteous (See Deut.28:1-14; 3Jn.2; Isa.1:18-19; Exo.15:26, 23:20-25). The Bible reveals that for each of the blessings to come man must fulfill certain conditions. This is what I am talking about. If you do your part, God will always fulfill His promises in your life. Just consider this verse;

"Bring all the tithes into the storehouse, That there may be food in My house, And try Me now in this,' Says the LORD of hosts, 'If I will not open for you the windows of heaven And pour out for you such blessing That there will not be room enough to receive it" (Mal.3:10).

Here there is one command and three blessings. The command is "Bring all the tithes into the store house." The blessings are, "Open heavens, release of the blessing, and divine supplies in abundance."

See this other one;

"Give, and it will be given to you: good measure, pressed down, shaken together, and running over will be put into your bosom. For with the same measure that you use, it will be measured back to you" (Luke 6:38).

The one command is simple "Give." Notice how Jesus Christ describes the covenant blessings that are released for the one who gives: "Given to you, good measure, pressed down, shaken together, running over, put into your bosom, proportionate to your measure."

We can conclude this point by saying that generous giving activates multidimensional blessings on our lives and families.

Parents bless your children:

One of the means by which covenant blessings are released is through parental blessings. Parents, especially fathers, occupy a divine office in the family. The office of a father is a divine office that represents God's authority in the family. When this office is abused, the children suffer enormously. How many children are laboring under curses which were released on them not by an enemy but by their parents at home? I witnessed a woman who pulled out her breast and showed to her child and then began to curse him. What do you think would have happened to this boy? Parents, I know sometimes your children can provoke you very badly. Please, God did not raise you to curse, but to bless people, so mind what you say when you are provoked by your children. Your tongue can build or destroy them. It can also give them life or death.

"Death and life are in the power of the tongue, And those who love it will eat its fruit" (Prov.18:21).

If you curse them, the curse will work on them and when they begin to agonize, you will join them to weep and mourn.

The patriarchs blessed their children:

Abraham, Isaac and Jacob were very conscious of the fact that the blessing of God was upon their lives. They also understood how to transfer the blessing onto their children. Many times in the Bible they blessed their children by laying their hands on them. In Genesis 27, Isaac decided to bless Esau when he began to sense that he was about to die. Before Jacob left home to travel abroad, his father Isaac laid hands on him and blessed him in the presence of his mother (Gen.28:1-4). No wonder God's hand was upon him wherever he went.

The idea of blessing children by parents was so common among the Jews, that in the days of Jesus Christ parents brought their children to Him for blessings (Mark 10:13-15). The question is, have you been blessing your children or cursing them? Generally, parents who do not bless their children find it easy to curse them.

Bless them today:

Today, lay your hands on your children and bless them from your heart. Why should you wait until when you are lying on your death bed before you begin to struggle to bless them? Do it now while all your senses are still alert.

The blessing is not a onetime affair. There are seasons

when the children need the blessing: When they are born, at dedication, when they are about to start school, at the start of every new school year, before they travel away from home, when they come back, before exams, when they are going out to write a public exam, when they are getting married, when they need favor, when they are under an attack, when they are facing challenges, when they need promotion, etc. You should discern when your children need the blessing and call them and bless them. When God revealed this to me, I resolved that yearly my father must lay hands on me. Whenever I travel out of the country, I meet with him for the blessing before I go. He will keep doing that till the day he will die.

Today, cancel the curses you have placed on your children. You cannot put a blessing on a curse. First forgive them and cancel the curses you had declared in the past consciously or unconsciously before you begin to bless them. Some of them may be very far; even abroad. Call them and bless them. Lay hands on those who are around and bless them. If you do not know what to say, use the following scriptures (Deut.28:1-14; Gen.24:60; Gen.27:28-29).

The blessing will break the curse:
The blessing is stronger than the curse. Use it to break curses on your children. One day in church God gave me a word of knowledge concerning a woman who was in the service. He told me to tell her to start to bless all her children instead of cursing them. I called her up and told her what God had said and I prayed for her family. Not long after that one of her sons who was a professional scammer came back home, repented and stopped scamming. Not long after that God

opened a door for the young man to travel to the USA for studies. After a few months this lady and her husband came to my office to present the tithe of their son's first salary. The young man had become very responsible. During the Power Must Change Hands program last year, I told parents to bless their children continuously for seven days. At the end, there were many testimonies from those who obeyed. Children were healed, transformed, and restored. A woman testified that a dark cloud left her daughter who before, could not read and she began to read and to reason well.

I believe that if you decide to engage the blessing against any curse that is working against your children, something new will happen to them.

Children do your part:

For the blessing to manifest in your life as a child, you must do the following:

1. Recognize parental authority:

Realize that your parents are a channel of divine blessings. God warns us to respect them, without which our days will be shortened (Eph.6:1-3). Sadly enough, some children disrespect their parents but go around looking for the most anointed prophet to bless them. It cannot work like that. First ensure that you have peace with your parents before you go out to look for blessings.

Your spiritual parents also have authority over you. Relate well with them so that God can always use them to bless you (Read Num.6:22-27). There are seasons in your life when you should go to your spiritual authorities for the blessing: when you are tired, when you need a breakthrough, when you are moving to the next level, before a battle, before an exam, before you marry, etc. May the Holy Spirit guide you.

2. Present gifts to them:

Isaac requested for a special meal from Esau before the blessing (Gen.27:1-10). He learned this from his father Abraham. Why present a gift? You must touch the heart of the one who carries the blessing in order to cause it flow. When we touch God's heart through our praise and worship, He blesses us (Ps.22:3, 66:5-6). We are not supposed to worship our parents whether they are alive or dead. The Bible says we should honor them (Eph.6:2). When you honor them, you touch their hearts. Even when you dishonor them you touch their hearts too. When they speak over you in such an atmosphere, the words affect you.

So this month, give them special gifts. You should never go to seek for a blessing empty handed. Whenever I honor my parents and they speak blessings on me, I see results. If in the past you had provoked your parents to curse you, this is the time to go to them and make peace.

Your labor in prayer alone cannot bring the fullness of the blessing on your life. After fasting and praying, step out and seek the blessing of your parents.

What about ungodly parents?

Ungodly parents here speak of those who do not worship the God of the Bible. Some of them worship idols. Even in this state, such parents still have authority over you. They are your parents and you MUST honor them. To honor them does not mean that you should join them in their idolatry. Please do not. Honor them by taking care of their needs. Talk

271

to them with respect. Visit them and make them happy. Even if they do not pronounce blessings on you, God will bless you. If you abandon them because you think that they are witches and wizards, God will not bless you. I used to wonder how the parents who did not kill you when you were a baby have suddenly become witches and wizard today when you are viable and can take care of them. Some children never give a franc to the same parents and relatives who sponsored them in school because they fear that they can be attacked spiritually. Please sit down and think over it again.

Give to God:

As you draw close to the end of this program, prepare a special offering to appreciate God for all that He is has done in your life during this program. By the grace of God every year on this mountain I review my giving. Any time God leads you to increase your giving you also increase in your receiving. A woman I met for the first time two months ago, testified to me that after Power Must Change Hands in 2011, she decided as inspired by the Holy Spirit to thank God with her one month's salary plus 10%. She shared the money to some pastors and some needy people. She said God blessed her with a business deal worth more than two million francs and it turned her life around. She said from that year she began to experience God as the God who answers prayers. According to her she had been in Church for years but had not known God like that. Whatever God tells you to do on this mountain, do it (Jn.2:5).

PRAYER POINTS
1. Thank God for the gift of family. Thank and praise God for your

parents, children, brothers, sisters, aunts, uncles, etc.

2. *Ask God to forgive you for being a bad example in any way in your family.*

3. *Consider carefully whether there is anyone in your family who has hurt you.*

4. *Forgive that person and decide to let go of the offense. Now pray, "Father, I forgive…for….I let go of the offense from my heart and I open my heart to him/her from today, in the name of Jesus.*

5. *Think carefully about your relationships in the family. Is there someone you have hurt in your family? Pray this pray, "Father, I repent of hurting …. (Mention the name and what you did). O Lord, forgive me and restore my relationship with …. In the name of Jesus.*

6. *Father, forgive me for cursing …. (Mention the name of your children, parents, relatives you have cursed), in the name of Jesus.*

7. *I withdraw any negative pronouncement I have made against myself, my children, my relatives, etc, in the name of Jesus (If there are some cases you know, please deal with them).*

8. *I cancel the curse with the blood of Jesus Christ.*

9. *I take authority over any evil spirit assigned to tear us apart. I bind you foul spirit and cast you out of my family, in the mighty name of Jesus.*

10. *I pull down all negative thoughts the devil has injected in*

11. *my heart against my children, parents, relatives, in the name of Jesus.*

12. *I use the blood of Jesus Christ to neutralize all accusing thoughts Satan has planted in the hearts of my parents/ children against me, in the name of Jesus.*

13. *I destroy any wall of separation raised by the devil between us, in the name of Jesus.*

14. *My Father, arise for the healing and restoration of my family, in*

the name of Jesus.

15. I believe that today is the day of restoration of lost blessings in my family. Father, let the door of multidimensional blessings open in my family, in the name of Jesus.

16. Father, on this mountain of restoration, restore all lost generational blessings in my family, in the name of Jesus.

17. Use the following scriptures and begin to pray for God's blessings on your life (Deut.28:1-14; Gen.24:60; Gen.27:28-29, Gen.49:25-26; Eph.3:15-21).

DAY 30

PRAISE AND THANKSGIVING

"Let the peoples praise You, O God; Let all the peoples praise You. Then the earth shall yield her increase; God, our own God, shall bless us. God shall bless us, And all the ends of the earth shall fear Him" (Ps.67:5-7).

To worship God is to appreciate Him for who He is. So today, appreciate Him by calling all His names that you know. Describe Him in the beauty of His holiness. May He put words in your mouth with which to paint the splendor of His majesty. On the other hand to praise God is to honor and appreciate Him for what He has done and for what He will do. During these thirty days, He has done mighty things in your life and family. He has opened doors that have been closed against you for generations. Everlasting blessings have been activated in your life, family, Church and the nation. King David in praise said,

"What shall I render to the LORD For all His benefits toward me?" (Ps.116:12).

Today, as you praise God, every blessing that has been activated in your life shall be established forever. This means that miracles shall be perfected in your life, in Jesus' name.

Today, we are not going to ask God for anything. We are going to minister to Him by sharing our testimonies and worshipping Him. Take time and praise Him. Testify about what He has done in your life during the prayer time.

Send us your testimonies today!

By SMS: (237) 674495895/ 699902618 or

By Email: voiceofrevivalcameroon@yahoo.com

I also encourage you to give God a thanksgiving sacrifice. This special offering is a gift to tell God that you appreciate Him for carrying you through this special season of fasting and prayer. You can also sow into the project the Lord has committed into our hands.

Pastor Godson and Family have relocated to Yaoundé to establish Christian Restoration Network, which is dedicated to the holistic restoration of individuals, families and the nations.

CRN is going to establish "Restoration Prayer Camp" in Yaoundé which will serve for retreats, research, and training agents of revival.

If God is impressing on your heart to be part of it, contact us through, **(237) 674495895/ 699902618**

or Email: voiceofrevivalcameroon@yahoo.com

BIBLE READING PLANS

READING THE NEW TESTAMENT IN 30 DAYS

1. Matthew 1-9
2. Matthew 10-15
3. Matthew 16-22
4. Matthew 23-28
5. Mark 1-8
6. Mark 9-16
7. Luke 1-6
8. Luke 7-11
9. Luke 12-18
10. Luke 19-24
11. John 1-7
12. John 8-13
13. John 14-21
14. Acts 1-7
15. Acts 8-14
16. Acts 15-21
17. Acts 22-28
18. Romans 1-8
19. Romans 9-16
20. 1 Corinthians 1-9
21. 1 Corinthians 10-16
22. Corinthians 1-13
23. Galatians - Ephesians
24. Philippians - 2 Thessalonians
25. 1 Timothy - Philemon
26. Hebrews
27. James - 2 Peter
28. 1 John - 3 John
29. Revelation 1-11
30. Revelation 12-22

READING THE GOSPELS IN 30 DAYS

1. Matthew 1-4
2. Matthew 5-10
3. Matthew 11-13
4. Matthew 14-16
5. Matthew 17-20
6. Matthew 21-24
7. Matthew 25-28
8. Mark 1-4
9. *Catch Up Day*
10. Mark 5-8
11. Mark 9-12
12. Mark 13-16
13. Luke 1-3
14. Luke 4-7
15. Luke 8-11
16. Luke 12-15
17. Luke 16-17
18. *Catch Up Day*
19. Luke 18-19
20. Luke 20-22
21. Luke 23-24
22. John 1-3
23. John 4-6
24. John 7-10
25. *Catch Up Day*
26. John 8-11
27. John 12-13
28. John 14-16
29. John 17-19
30. John 20-21

OTHER CHRISTIAN RESTORATION NETWORK PUBLICATIONS:

- ❖ Power Must Change Hands Vol.1: Dealing with Evil Foundations
- ❖ Power Must Change Hands Vol.2: Pursue Overtake and Recover All
- ❖ Power Must Change Hands Vol.3: Jesus Christ Must Reign
- ❖ Power Must Change Hands Vol.4: Arise and Shine
- ❖ Praying Like Jesus
- ❖ Conquering the Giant Called Poverty
- ❖ Generous Living
- ❖ Prayer Storm Book 1: Bind the Strongman
- ❖ Prayer Storm Book 2: Personal and Family Deliverance for You
- ❖ A Difference by Fire
- ❖ Your Time for Divine Expansion
- ❖ Jesus Our Jubilee
- ❖ The Choice of a Friend
- ❖ Christians and Politics
- ❖ Prayer Storm Daily Prayer Guide (monthly devotional)

For copies, contact your local books store or direct your request to:

Prayer Storm Team
P.O. Box 5018
Nkwen, Bamenda
Tel.: (237) 679465717 or 677436964
godsontnembo@gmail.com